Learning to Speak ACT

Copyright © 2017 by Chris Cho

ISBN 978 – 1 – 387 – 08221 – 6

All rights reserved. Any unauthorized reprint or use of this material is prohibited. No part of this book may be reproduced or transmitted in any form or by any means, electronic or mechanical, including photocopying, recording, or by any information storage and retrieval system without express written permission from the author.

Please note: ACT is a registered trademark of ACT, Inc. , which was not involved in the production of, and does not endorse, this product.

This book is dedicated to my parents.

They taught me to dream, and more importantly, gave me the ability to fulfill those dreams.

Our Covenant

I agree to provide you with the highest quality information that will ever be produced.

You agree to enjoy life a touch more than maybe you were prior to reading this book.

Now we are in this thing together.

#OnlyHardWork
@chrisXcho

Hello My Friend,

You don't know how excited I am to be writing this.

I have a dream. It is a simple one. My dream is to give you the *choice* to make your dream not a dream.

If your dream is to attend a specific college, then let's make that dream happen by allowing you to earn the ACT score that will get you in to that college. If your dream is to attend a specific college, but the standard tuition is a touch too ridiculous, then let's make that dream happen by allowing you to earn the ACT score that leads to a merit scholarship.

As long as you have any sort of dream that involves college in some sort of way, then let me now assure you that you have purchased the one book that you really needed to get. Basically everything I know about the ACT is in this book. And fortunately for you, what I know about the ACT is basically everything.

Dreams that become reality are the dreams that this book was built for.

I think we're ready.

Hell yeah.

Table of Contents

- **QUESTIONS OF THE WEEK** 15
- **Don't Go In Order: An LTSA Mantra** 17

English

- **Four Mantras** 21
  1. Shorter is Better 21
  2. Don't Be Repetitive 21
  3. Avoid Unnecessary Punctuation 21
  4. No Slang, Informal, or Creative Language 22

- **Seven Punctuation Points** 23
  1. Semicolons 23
  2. Dashes 23
  3. Commas 23
  4. Apostrophes 24
  5. Parentheses 24
  6. Colons 25
  7. Something to Memorize 26

- **Things You MUST Memorize** 27

- **Things You Should TRY to Memorize** 31

- **Things You CHOOSE to Memorize** 35

- **Thirteen Specialty Questions** 40
  1. The Yes/No Question (YN) 40
  2. The A to D Question (AD) 41
  3. The Addition Question (AQ) 43
  4. The Homophone Question (HQ) 44
  5. The Sentence Re-Arrangement Question (SR) 46
  6. The NOT Question (NQ) 48
  7. The Transition Word/Phrase Question (TW) 49
  8. The Keep/Delete Question (KD) 51
  9. The Divide the Paragraph Question (DP) 52
  10. The Vocab-ish Question (VQ) 53
  11. The If-Delete Question (ID) 54
  12. The Add a Sentence Question (AS) 55
  13. The Other Instructions Question (OI) 56

- **Three English Meditations** 59
  1. A Monster Start 59
  2. Warm Up Your Brain 59
  3. One Time Check 60

- **Targets & Expectations** 61

Math

▶ **Three Mantras** 65
　1. Skip Around 65
　2. Don't Skip Steps 65
　3. Be Flexible 66

▶ **Four Alternatives to Standard Math** 67
　1. Use the Given Answers (UGA) 67
　2. Draw Your Own Diagram (DOD) 67
　3. Substitute Your Own Numbers (SYON) 68
　4. Trial & Error (TE) 68

▶ **Things You MUST Memorize** 69

▶ **Things You Should TRY to Memorize** 75

▶ **Things You CHOOSE to Memorize** 83

▶ **Five Reasons to Skip** 88
　1. Because it's a "cluster block" (CB) 88
　2. Because of the type 89
　3. Because of its setup 89
　4. Because it's 3-D geometry 89
　5. Because it's unfamiliar or uncomfortable 90

▶ **Seven Math Meditations** 91
　1. The First 20 91
　2. Embrace Your Weakness 91
　3. Expect Oddballs 92
　4. One More Step 92
　5. A Capped Out "NOT" 92
　6. The Wording Matters 93
　7. The Last 10 93

▶ **Targets & Expectations** 94

Reading

- **Four Mantras** 99
    1. Choose Your Order 99
    2. Bail As Needed 99
    3. Write Notes 100
    4. Trust Yourself 101

- **Find Your Balance** 102

- **Things You MUST Memorize** 104

- **Things You Should TRY to Memorize** 106

- **Things You CHOOSE to Memorize** 108

- **Four Specialty Questions** 110
    1. The "most nearly means" Question (MNM) ... 110
    2. The Main Purpose/Idea Question (MP) ... 111
    3. The Paragraph Question (PQ) 112
    4. The Agree Question (AQ) 112

- **Nine Reading Meditations** 114
    1. Passage A/Passage B 114
    2. Tone 114
    3. Don't Rush 115
    4. Be Efficient and Decisive 115
    5. Know Yourself 115
    6. Practicing the "Why" 116
    7. Ignore What You Don't Know 116
    8. Know If You're Beat 117
    9. One Time Check 117

- **Targets & Expectations** 119

Science

- **Four Mantras** **125**
  1. Not Trying to Trick You 125
  2. Don't Read Until Necessary 125
  3. Be Max Out Efficient 125
  4. Mark It Up 125

- **The Core Roadmap** **126**
  1. Wave 1 (W1) 126
  2. All Text (AT) 127
  3. Wave 2 (W2) 127
  4. Random Guessing (RG) 127
  5. Wave 3 (W3) 128
  6. The Road to 27 128

- **The AT Passage** **131**

- **Things You Must Memorize** **133**

- **Things You Should TRY to Memorize** **136**

- **Things You CHOOSE to Memorize** **137**

- **Six Specialty Questions** **138**
  1. Split Questions (SQ) 138
  2. Column Questions (CQ) 140
  3. Extrapolation Questions (EQ) 141
  4. In-Between Questions (IB) 142
  5. Science-Sense Questions (SS) 143
  6. Fact Questions (FQ) 144

- **Seven Science Meditations** **147**
  1. Scan, Don't Read 147
  2. Ignore Baseline Material 147
  3. The Axes Matter 148
  4. Eliminate As You Can 148
  5. Oddball Passages are W2s 148
  6. Know If You're Beat 149
  7. You Can't Go Faster Than You Can Go 149

- **Targets & Expectations** **150**

The Essay

▶ **The Essay** ... 155

▶ **Things You MUST Memorize** ... 156

▶ **Things You CHOOSE to Memorize** ... 159

Closing Remarks

▶ **Four Final Meditations** ... 165
  1. What Clock? ... 165
  2. Practice Tests ... 165
  3. Just One Piece ... 166
  4. Find YOUR Path ... 166

▶ **Coming Soon: LTSA Live** ... 167

▶ **Epilogue** ... 169

▶ **Endorsements** ... 171

LTSA Questions of the Week

Before we get into the content of this book, I would like to introduce you to the LTSA email subscription.

What is LTSA Questions of the Week?

LTSA Questions of the Week is a weekly email that will allow you to check your fluency in ACT. Within this email LTSA questions will both reinforce and troubleshoot material that you will learn from this book. Tackling the questions on a weekly basis will keep you razor sharp and help you clarify what areas within the ACT may need more or less of your attention. With every **QOTW** set, there will also be detailed explanations that will fluidly mesh with the content of this book.

Simultaneously reading through *Learning to Speak ACT* and working through the **QOTW** forms a cohesive plan to systematically dissect the many facts, strategies, and nuances that underpin the ACT.

How to subscribe to the LTSA Questions of the Week:

Send an email to **Subscribe@LearningtoSpeakACT.com** that includes your **First and Last name**, your **direct email address**.

To be sure you don't miss an email, add **QOTW@LearningtoSpeakACT.com** to your address book.

Requests:

Do you have a request for a topic to be addressed in the next QOTW email? If so, send it to **Requests@LearningtoSpeakACT.com**

Don't Go In Order: An LTSA Mantra

I tend to be direct. When a student asks me if I think he can achieve a certain ACT score, it just doesn't make sense to be anything but direct. I will say "yes", if I believe he can. And I will most certainly say "no" if the student is simply not working hard enough to *earn* the score that he asked me about.

In keeping with my general proclivity toward being direct, let me know proclaim: anyone who takes the ACT and actually does all of the questions in order is a sucker.

Very simply, standardized tests like the ACT were not designed to be done in order, and this idea applies to basically every section of the test.

Why bring this up now?

Because the idea of NOT going in order also applies to how you should also read LTSA.

At the start of each major unit of the book, **there are Mantras, and these items are the first things you should start to flat out memorize.** To be crystal clear, I am advising you to **NOT just start reading the entire English portion** of this book, simply because the English part is the first of the four major parts. Instead, **you should read through the Mantras of each of the four major parts.**

What should you read after you've read the Mantras? Now, **you should read everything between the Mantras and the end of what you'll see is entitled "Things You MUST Memorize".** Again, to be crystal clear, within the English portion of the book, you should then read everything from pages 23-30. In the Math portion of the book, read everything from pages 67-74. In Reading, read everything from pages 102-105, and in Science, read the very key pages from 125-134.

With all of that awesome material now starting to circulate through your brain, **head to the Meditations** that you will see toward the end of each major part of the book. After you read through the Meditations, you have a couple of routes that you could choose, each of which will obviously continue to guide you smoothly through your ACT journey.

You could **start to work your way through the "Things You Should TRY to Memorize".** This is the material that is the next level up from what you "MUST" memorize. **Alternatively, you could start to work your way through any "Specialty Questions" that appear toward the end of a given major section of the book.** Taking either route is great, so don't stress about the decision you end up making. Go with what makes you feel more confident and comfortable.

When you make the decision to try to crush the ACT, you have made the decision to basically learn a new language. And to learn that language effectively, you need to build your skill set in stages. So please adhere to all that has been mentioned here. **Know the Mantras, inside and out. Memorize things that *must* be memorized. Get your mind calibrated by reading through some key Meditations.** And from there, then keep building and pushing forward.

Ready?

Let's go.

English

Four Mantras

1) Shorter is Better

On test day, it should cross your mind that you are going to pick a given answer simply because it is the shortest and most direct option listed.

The idea of *shorter is better* might cross your mind three or four times within a given English section. The idea might cross your mind even more times. If the idea doesn't end up crossing your mind at all, then something very strange is happening.

2) Don't Be Repetitive

For some students, it will seem very similar to the idea of *shorter is better* to also say *don't be repetitive*. But I also know that for some students, this idea will seem like a separate thought.

So just to be sure that all students are being helped, let me take a brief moment to acknowledge that if you notice that something is repetitive within a given answer choice, you would have a great reason to cross that answer out.

3) Avoid Unnecessary Punctuation

Soon enough, we will be talking about punctuation.
For now, I just want to plant a seed.

Once you know when to use certain key punctuation items, you should be well-equipped to also know when NOT to use certain punctuation items.

And so on test day, do not be surprised if you end up choosing an answer or two that has either no punctuation at all or has less punctuation than was originally offered up to you.

4. No Slang, Informal, or Creative Language

Slang would be saying something like "would of", when what you really meant to say was "would have".

Informal would be calling something a "drag" or referring to a group of items as a "bunch of stuff".

Creative language would include metaphors and similes. So saying the ACT is a bigger challenge than running a marathon in flip-flops would be the kind of thing you would NOT expect in a correct ACT answer.

Veer away from options that have slang, options that seem informal, and options that seem to employ creative language.

And just like that, we are off to a smooth start within our English discussion my friend!

Seven Punctuation Points

You absolutely need to flat out memorize the basics of semicolons, dashes, commas, and apostrophes. You won't likely see many questions dealing with parentheses on test day, but you should probably pick up the straightforward information about it. I'll leave it to you to decide whether you are also going to get comfortable with what many would consider a trickier punctuation item: the colon.

Your dream is not the same as another's. The bigger the dream, the more knowledge you need to have. See what we are doing as a series of choices my friend. Some will choose to memorize nearly everything in this book; others will understand that they do not need to. It's totally ok if you're not sure which path you want to walk yet. Maybe we should let some of the information itself help you decide. Let's go.

1. semicolons (;)

A semicolon separates two full sentences.

> Ex.   I love soccer; the weather in Santa Monica is extraordinary.

2. dashes (-)

First, dashes usually come in pairs.

Please note the use of the word *usually*. I am not saying they always come in pairs, but they usually do.

Second, dashes act just like commas.

> Ex.   Soccer - the world's most popular sport - is gaining traction in the U.S.

3. commas (,)

Commas have a wide range of uses, and the ACT employs quite a few of those uses within its exams. For now, I want to introduce you to only some core concepts. As we get deeper into the book, you'll most certainly have the opportunity to learn even more fun stuff about commas.

One classic use of commas is to set off a description.

> Ex.   Soccer, the world's most popular sport, is gaining traction in the U.S.

So now you see why it was mentioned above that dashes act just like commas. Hopefully, you can also see what I just meant when I said that commas can set off a description.

A second thing to mention about commas right now is that when a pair of commas is being properly used, what is between the commas should typically be able to be removed from the sentence, and what is left still forms a normal sentence.

So in the given example, if we took out what was between the commas, "the world's most popular sport", what remains would still read like a normal sentence. "Soccer is gaining traction in the U.S."

A third thing to mention is that when used with conjunctions like "and" or "but", the comma will be placed in front of the conjunction.

    Ex.   I love soccer, and I hope the World Cup comes to the U.S. in 2026.

You probably already knew this last one, but it pays to be thorough my friend.

4 apostrophes (')

When apostrophes are being tested within the ACT, all you should likely need to know is how they act in regards to whether a given noun is possessive.

Let's now acknowledge that when an apostrophe comes BEFORE an "s", then the situation would be *singular possessive*.

    Ex.   The player's shirt was torn during the match he played yesterday.

In contrast, if an apostrophe comes AFTER an "s", then the situation would be *plural possessive*.

    Ex.   The players' shirts were torn during the match they played yesterday.

If you are having trouble deciding whether or not a situation even requires an apostrophe, try reversing things and using the word "of". For instance, if you were not sure in the first example as to whether or not a possessive situation was in play, you could take the word after the word with the apostrophe and ask yourself if that item is "of" the word with the apostrophe.

So in this case, you could ask yourself, "Is it the shirt 'of' the player"? When this type of statement makes sense, then the situation is possessive. If asking yourself such a question does not sound like it makes sense, then it is likely because there is nothing possessive within the given situation.

5 parentheses ()

Parentheses - just like dashes - act like commas.

So we have another form of punctuation that can be used to *describe*.

    Ex.   My beloved dogs (Fofa and Toby) live very happily with my ex-wife.

The slight difference between parentheses and dashes and commas is that parentheses do always come in pairs.

I imagine (and I hope) you didn't really need to be told that, but I had to say it for the sake of thoroughness.

6 colons (:)

If you think that colons are for lists, you need to get that out of your head. A list can involve a colon, but colons and lists do NOT go hand in hand.

Here's what I need you to know for the ACT.

Colons further *elaborate* on what was just said before the colon.

    Ex.   I live by a simple philosophy: no off days.

Hopefully, you can see within that example that the "no off days" part was *elaborating* on what my philosophy is.

A second idea you can keep in mind is that a properly used colon should also indicate a natural pause if you were speaking the sentence aloud.

7 Something to memorize...

Let's close out this discussion on punctuation by giving you a very specific potential question style to flat out memorize.

Imagine you are given the following options on test day.

A) capybara. She

B) capybara: she

C) capybara; she

D) capybara, she

The first thing I want you to notice is that the words are the same within each answer choice. Having acknowledged that, if you were wondering what the grammatical difference would be between option (A) and option (C), you would be right to wonder.

The difference between them is nothing. If the words are the same within given answer choices, and the only difference is that one uses a period and the other uses a semicolon, there is NO grammatical difference between them. Therefore, in this situation, you would be 100% justified in crossing out both options. It would be impossible to choose one over the other.

Now it's time to talk about a pattern that currently seems to be a thing within standardized tests. Please keep in mind that this is a pattern and NOT a fact.

But a legit pattern that seems to have been running through the ACT for quite a long time is that when there are two options, one with a period and one with a semicolon, the correct answer ends up being the one with the comma. So in this case, I am telling you that the pattern would lean us toward choosing option (D).

I don't know why this is a pattern; I just know that it has been one, and I think it might continue to be one for quite some time. The nice thing about standardized tests is that, by definition, they kind of need to be "standardized". I suppose this is why certain styles of questions and certain patterns just keep repeating. And this is precisely why beating an exam like the ACT is primarily about time, diligence, and experience.

Hope you noticed, by the way, all the killer punctuation I dropped in that previous paragraph. On that note, let's head into some crucial material that you flat out need to memorize.

Things You MUST Memorize

With some key punctuation foundations now in place, we can begin to sift through some information that you really do need to just memorize, hence the title of this part of the book.

Here's the deal: if you're not going to commit to memorizing what's about to follow on the next couple of pages or so, then it's kind of weird to even be reading this book.

Do you want to go to college? Do you want to save some potentially serious money when it comes to college?

If you answered "yes" to either question, then memorize all of the ensuing material within this part of the book. If you answered "no" to both questions, then literally set this book on fire.

1. "being"

If you see this word within a given answer choice, the likelihood that the choice is the correct answer is super, super small.

Why is this a thing?

Well, a semi-formal answer is because the word is typically part of passive constructions, which generally do not constitute strong ACT answers.

A less formal answer: who cares why it is a thing.

There was a recent exception to this pattern by the way. That exception probably means that a correct answer with "being" in it won't roll around again for another decade. And you can trust my friend that I am constantly monitoring what the ACT publishes, so I can keep you as up to date and clued in as possible.

2. "you"

I think we're all still taught never to use this word in a high school essay. Well here's the thing, the ACT isn't a high school essay. The ACT is its own animal, and what you need to know about it is, often times, specific to just the ACT.

On that note, let's acknowledge that you will know to choose "you" in a correct answer, if you see that it has already been used somewhere else in the sentence or the paragraph that a given English question is a part of.

    Ex.   If *you* want to do well on the ACT, then *you* should read this book.

This idea certainly extends to the use of the words "yourself" and "your" as well.

> Ex. If *you* are heading to Southern California, then it makes sense that *your* travel plans should include a stop in Santa Monica.

❸ s-verbs

Verbs that end in an "s" are SINGULAR. Whereas verbs that don't end in "s" are PLURAL.

This can be a bit counterintuitive, since nouns that end in "s" are plural.

If you happen to forget which one is which, in regards to verbs, use your own name in a sentence.

> Ex. Hayley *plays* field hockey.

Notice that the verb that should have naturally sounded right is one that would end in an "s", because, again, a SINGULAR verb ends with an "s".

❹ Parallelism

Whether you ever use the term *parallelism* or not is not a big deal. Recognizing it when you see it is the more important thing to be able to pull off on test day.

A classic example of what parallelism can look like is when you keep the form of a string of verbs the same.

> Ex. I enjoy *helping* my students, *listening* to new music, and *eating* great food.

As you can see from the italicized words, all of the verbs end in "-ing".

> Ex. I enjoy *to help* my students, *to listen* to new music, and *to eat* great food.

This example is another good example of parallelism, but in this case, I used the word "to" in front of each verb.

Neither example is better than the other. The idea is that in both cases, the form of the verbs is maintained.

> Ex. I enjoy national soccer matches *for their* high levels of intensity and *for their* significance to the players.

In this third example, you can also see that parallelism can be illustrated by the repetition of a specific phrase. This illustration of parallelism could seem to go against Mantra #2, so it would be understandable if at first you were hesitant to select an option with this type of parallelism. But if you did notice that a specific phrase was being repeated like the example above, you would want that sort of repetition. So to be clear, in this instance, a good example of parallelism would beat out a concern regarding repetition.

5) The "DELETE" Option

Every so often you will be given the answer option to "DELETE" the underlined portion of a given question.

The most likely reason to choose this option as the correct answer is because what is underlined is REPETITIVE. This isn't the only reason to potentially choose the DELETE option, but, as stated, it is the most likely reason.

6) The "Occupation" Question

The name of this is certainly not a formal grammar term; it's just what I got accustomed to calling this situation that appears within the English section with a good degree of regularity.

If you state what a person does, her *occupation*, BEFORE the person's name, then you will use NO COMMAS.

>   Ex.   The exploits of the renowned scientist and masterful rhetorician Gianna have been well established.

On the other hand, if you state what a person does AFTER the person's name, then you will use TWO COMMAS.

>   Ex.   The exploits of Gianna, the renowned scientist and masterful rhetorician, have been well established.

Like so many things that we will talk about within the confines of the ACT, I don't know why this is a thing. I just know it's a thing. And it's a thing that you should simply flat out memorize.

7. The "3/4 Transitions" Question

This is a very well-established pattern within the ACT. However, keep in mind that I did just mention that it is a pattern, versus a fact. It is possible that the ACT could change from some of its established patterns. Happily, it just seems like the ACT isn't really interested in doing so.

If three of the four options have a transition word/phrase and the remaining answer option does not have a transition word/phrase, then the correct answer is extremely likely to be the one *without* the transition word/phrase.

> Ex.
> - F) Regardless, Danielle
> - G) On the other hand, Danielle
> - H) In addition to, Danielle
> - J) Danielle

So in that hypothetical answer option set, I am telling you to choose option (J). I don't believe I have ever seen this pattern not hold up. You can be sure that I am diligently checking all published material to be sure, but for now my friend, I can assure you that it is very, very safe to trust this idea.

Things You Should TRY to Memorize

It is simply a fact that we are not all capable of memorizing the same amount of material. And for whatever reasons, for each of us, some things stick better in our heads than other things. For instance, I have always had a strong ability to memorize people's names. On the other hand, when I took physics back in high school, nothing I seemed to "study" ever seemed to stay in my head.

Essentially, what I am now trying to tell you is that it would be amazing if you could memorize nearly everything that is about to come within this next part of the book. But if you try to memorize it all, and not everything ends up sticking, good things are still afoot my friend.

That said, like the title of this part of the states, *try* to memorize everything.

1. Run-Ons

A run-on is a classic error in grammar. A run-on is when you combine two full sentences with a comma. There is pretty much going to be at least one run-on tucked away somewhere within every English section of the ACT.

>   Ex.   I love soccer, it is an amazing sport.

Notice that what is before the comma and what is after the comma are both full sentences.

There are quite a few ways to correct a run-on, so for now, let's introduce one classic go-to way that the ACT employs, which is to change the punctuation.

>   Ex.   I love soccer; it is an amazing sport.

This revised example is now a proper sentence, which I imagine may not surprise you given our earlier punctuation discussion. So the first way that I want you to know how to correct a run-on is to swap the incorrect comma for a correct semicolon.

2. Six Classic Linking Verbs

Here are six classic linking verbs:

>   is / are   was / were   has / have

I always write them in pairs, because they naturally come in pairs, with the item on the left being the singular item, while the item on the right is the plural one.

Now let's acknowledge a pattern within the ACT.

If one of the six classic linking verbs is what is originally given, and you notice that its partner is among the answer choices, then it is extremely likely that the correct answer is either the original option or its partner.

For example, if "have" was what was originally given, and "has" is one of the other options, I want you thinking that one of those two answer choices is almost definitely the correct answer. So I am basically telling you to likely ignore the other two options.

The idea behind this is that when the ACT chooses to give you a classic pair among these six linking verbs, choosing between that pair is what the ACT is choosing to test you on.

③ Identifying the Subject

Building off of the last point, let's now talk about how to potentially identify the subject of a given sentence, which is how you will likely know whether a given verb should be singular or plural.

One classic way to identify a subject is to look for a preposition.

Prepositions are small connecting words like "to", "from", "in", "with", and "on".

If you spot a preposition, then the subject of a sentence very, very often is what is right BEFORE the preposition.

    Ex.   A group of my friends *is* coming over to watch the match.

This is a great example of how misleading some sentences can initially be. Many would think that the example above is grammatically incorrect. Many would think that the "is" should be an "are".

But if you notice the preposition "of", that word will tip you off that the subject of the sentence is the "group", which is singular, which is why the proper linking verb to use is the "is".

A second classic way to identify a subject is to notice a phrase that is bracketed by commas.

If you see such a phrase, then the subject should be what comes before the phrase that is bracketed by the commas.

    Ex.   My family, which is composed of many members, is a friendly bunch.

Again, initially, this could be a tricky situation. But once you know to potentially notice the phrase between the commas, you're almost definitely in really strong shape.

The subject within this sentence is the singular "family", which is again why the "is" is the proper singular verb.

4. IDP

You should likely have noticed by now that this book strives to veer from formality and just more practically teach you things that will straight up make you more powerful on test day.

So, "IDP" is the acronym I use for something I got into the habit of calling an *introductory descriptive phrase*.

The idea is that when you start a sentence by describing someone or something, the someone or something needs to come right after the comma that comes at the end of the IDP.

    Ex.   Having read this book, you will feel confident on test day.

So the IDP is the opening part of the sentence, which in this case, is describing the "you" in the sentence.

To hopefully make this point even clearer, here is an incorrect example of using an IDP.

    Ex.   Having read this book, the test seemed more manageable.

This incorrect sentence is making it seem like "the test" read this book.

As a final, very ACT-specific comment, an IDP that begins with a verb that ends in "-ing" is almost definitely describing a person. So if you see an IDP that begins with a verb that ends in "-ing", what is after the comma should very likely be a person.

5. "whom"

A classic way to know if the word "whom" is being correctly used within a standardized test question is to see if there is a *preposition* right in front of it.

    Ex.   This notebook belongs *to* whom.

It is not that a preposition is required to be present in order to use the word 'whom', it is simply how nearly any ACT question would likely be written if 'whom' ended up being part of the correct answer.

    Ex.   *For* whom was this book intended?

6. Double-Comma Words

Some words, when they appear in the middle of a sentence, require two commas, one in front and one in back.

    Ex.   One of the many skills, *for instance*, that a well-trained student possesses is the ability to recognize what she does and does not know.

In this example, I am highlighting that "for instance" is one of the phrases that require the double-comma treatment.

Here are the current words and phrases that the ACT has used that have required double commas.

for example   *for instance*   *however*   *instead*   *though*

7 The Pronoun Question

This is a pattern that is basically a 100% lock.

If you three of the four answer options are pronouns and one answer is longer, but that answer *specifies* what the pronouns in the other options were potentially referring to, then the correct answer is the longer answer option.

> Ex. F) it
> G) them
> H) the family of capybaras
> J) some

This pattern is a very specific time that we are going against English Mantra #1: Shorter is Better. If you care, the basic reason why is that the pronouns do not make it clear enough what is getting referred to within the given sentence, making the longer, more specific answer, necessary.

If you don't really care, and you just memorize this as a pattern, then welcome to the very practical world of training to crush the ACT!

8 A Comma between Adjectives

Another necessary time to use a comma would be between two adjectives.

> Ex. The charming, intelligent Hayley had her choice of colleges after earning her great test score.

In this case, the comma that is between "charming" and "intelligent" is necessary because it is properly separating two adjectives.

If you find yourself in a situation in which you cannot tell if a word is an adjective, trying saying the word "is" right before the word. Typically, an adjective will sound very smooth coming after the word "is". Whereas, other parts of speech can sound a bit awkward if you said them after the word "is".

> Ex. Hayley *is* charming   &   Hayley *is* intelligent

Things You CHOOSE to Memorize

Now we are entering the realm of material that I need you to understand just how much control you have over your own ACT destiny.

If you are trying to obliterate the exam, I am giving you a blueprint to do so. And it should be obvious what you now need to do: *choose* to continue memorizing as much of this English information as possible.

If you are trying to get past the ACT, but not necessarily trying to alter your universe with your ACT score, then I think it'd be super smart to read everything that is about to follow. But I think I am making it fairly clear that your college dreams will not be devastated if you do not acquire everything that is about to follow.

1. The S-Verb Question

Let's combine a couple of things we discussed earlier and see if we can get you ready for a question that has a very solid probability of appearing on any given exam.

We have discussed how a verb that ends in an "s" is a singular verb and that a verb that does not end in an "s" is a plural verb. Let's combine this fact with what seems to be another pattern within the exam.

If the original option within a given question is a verb that does or does not end in an "s", AND its partner, the one with or without an "s" is one of the other options, then one of those two is almost definitely the correct answer.

    A) employs

    B) has been employing

    C) was employed

    D) employ

In the set of options above, I am basically telling you that the correct answer will either be option (A) or option (D). The reasoning behind this is simply that when the ACT gives you both options, what you are almost definitely being tested on is singular versus plural, versus considering the tense of the verb. (If this sounds like something we spoke about when we were talking about the classic linking verbs, you're right, it should.)

So, if on a given question, you were not sure which item to choose, at least you would be down to what should be an extremely effective 50-50 guess.

That said, ideally, you will know what the subject of a given sentence is and you will concretely know whether you need the s-verb or the verb without the "s". And certainly, it could be quite likely that you could use the ideas we discussed in regards to how to identify a subject to properly determine which verb you need for a given question.

2) Starting with a Person

This is a pattern that is definitely NOT 100%, but it's pretty darn close. So if you're not sure what to do, trust this pattern.

If there is one, and only one, answer that begins with a person, that is likely the correct answer. This is a bit of a play on the grammar idea of active voice versus passive voice, which is not something that I think you need to be overly concerned about at this juncture in your preparation.

      Ex.   A)   the game is something
                  B)   she was thinking
                  C)   her intention was to
                  D)   that was something that she

So in this example, the pattern dictates choosing option (B) as the correct answer.

When this pattern is active, it is quite likely that the *person* we will see will be in the form of a pronoun, such as "she", "he", or "they". And keep in mind that a pronoun like "her" is not clearly indicating a person. In option (C), for instance, what is really being referenced is 'her intention', which is not a person, but a thing.

As a final disclaimer, if you think you see an exception to this pattern on test day, you should almost definitely trust yourself.

3) Splitting Into 2 Sentences

This is another pattern that is not a 100% lock, but it is very, very reliable.

If there is one, and only one, option that splits what's given into two sentences, that should be your correct answer.

      Ex.   A)   into a great ending, however, it is likely
                  B)   into a great ending. It is likely
                  C)   into a great ending
                  D)   into a great ending that was

So the pattern we are acknowledging here is dictating that the answer to choose is option (B). Why is this a pattern on the ACT? Probably because splitting a given sentence into two sentences eliminates what was a very big, bulky sentence.

Again, this isn't a 100% thing. But it is pretty much a 99% thing. Trusting every pattern mentioned in LTSA is likely a very, very safe thing to do. But if you are trying to get every question right on test day, then don't take every pattern for granted as being a locked thing.

4 "few" versus "little" & "many" versus "much"

Words like "few" and "many" are used for when you are referring to things that can be counted.

> Ex.   How *many* quarters do I need for the meter?

> Ex.   He has seen *fewer* movies than his friend.

Words like "little" and "much" are used for when you are referring to things that cannot be counted.

> Ex.   How *much* homework do you have?

> Ex.   How *little* ketchup is still in the bottle?

5 4 Word Pairs

Certain words trigger the use of another word later within the same sentence.

> Ex.   I am *either* going to eat a salad *or* going to heat up some soup.

In this example, we see the classic pairing of "either" and "or".

Here are the four word pairs that you should likely just memorize.

> *either.......or*
> *neither.......nor*
> *between.......and*
> *not only.......but also*

> Ex.   It is *not only* important to memorize certain key facts, *but* it is *also* critical to learn patterns and tendencies of an exam like the SAT.

From this second example, you can see the key words within a pairing do not necessarily need to be right next to each other, but they do need to be present.

As a final comment, for the particular pair of neither/nor, it would be super strange, if not actually grammatically impossible, to see a "nor" without a "neither" having already been established. A sentence could certainly have an "or" and not have an "either" before it. But the same cannot be said for the neither/nor combo.

6. A Required Antecedent

A pronoun that is not part of what is underlined within a given sentence/question could force you to adjust what was underlined.

The idea here is that a pronoun within a given sentence needs to clearly be referring to something.

> Ex. The may qualm _for the people who attended the party_ is that there was not enough food for all of them.

If you were given the option to DELETE what was underlined, it would be a mistake to do so, because we would no longer know who the "them" at the end of the sentence was referring to.

7. A Quirk about "-ing" Verbs

Something particular to the world of standardized tests is that answer choices that use "-ing" verbs often times do not form full sentences. This is why, in a good number of scenarios, answers with "-ing" verbs will not end up being correct answers.

This is definitely a subtle point, so if it doesn't stick, no worries my friend. And definitely even fewer worries if the next, and final, item isn't something you love either.

8. A Funky "which"

This is definitely not a major point, which is why it is the final thing we are going to talk about before we head into the much more important specialty question that are about to be discussed.

The word "which" could be used to create something that isn't supposed to be a sentence by itself. This could be a helpful thing to know particularly when you are dealing with a potential run-on sentence, or if you were dealing with a clause that was supposed to be in between two commas, which should basically never be a full sentence either.

> Ex. The best sport in the world is football, Americans refer to it as soccer.

This is a classic run-on (which you should know from reading the previous part of the English portion of this book!) If we were to insert the word "which", what would be after the commas would no longer be a separate sentence, which would correct the run-on.

>   Ex.   The best sport in the word is football, *which* Americans refer to as soccer.

If this final point didn't make a lot of sense, it really is ok. This is a rather funky point that I am throwing in here for the sake of being absurdly thorough for my most hard-core students. Be assured, whatever dream you are trying to make real, it is extraordinarily unlikely for it to be resting on your understanding of this item.

9. which/that vs. who/whom

A way simpler thing to learn about the word "which" is that it is used to reference *things*. The same can be said for the word "that".

In contrast, the words "who" and "whom" are used to reference people.

>   Ex.   The team *that* comes in first will win a trophy.

In the example above, even though a team is made up of people, the team itself is still a thing, hence the word "that" would be the correct word to use, versus using the word "who".

10. "as"

When you use the word "as" to make a comparison, you should use it twice.

>   Ex.   Kaitlyn is *as* charming a person *as* I have ever met.

Thirteen Specialty Questions

I imagine that as you are reading this part of the book, some key facts are already nicely settling into place. I also imagine that you are starting to get familiar with the idea that there really are very consistent patterns within the English portion of the ACT.

This is why I have stated on countless occasions that the ACT English section is the most preparable part of any existing standardized test. The ACT seems to just keep repeating certain ideas, and wonderfully, this definitely extends to particular types of questions.

Dreams are great. Making your dream a reality is extraordinary. Let's keep making that happen by outlining the various classic types of questions that you will encounter within the first section of the ACT.

❶ *The Yes/No Question (YN)*

Potential Frequency:

It would seem like you can anticipate seeing this type of question on the day of your exam two or three times.

Priority Level:

Given that we know that this question is a staple to the exam, and that what you need to do and know about it is nothing heavy duty, flat out, you need to know what is about to be said.

Fundamental Idea/Approach:

This question will be incredibly simple to recognize. When it gets asked, it will always be the final question within a given block of questions. And the four answer options will always be split between two that start with "Yes" and two that start with "No".

The basic idea of the question is to ask you whether or not a given passage accomplished a particular goal. The basic approach to the question does not require anything crazy to do.

As you were doing the questions leading up to a potential YN at the end of a passage, you should have been reading every line, paying decent attention to what the passage was about. English passages tend to be light reading, so knowing what a passage was generally about should not likely be much of an issue.

Therefore, when you get to a potential YN, it would generally be very much expected that you already have an impulse regarding whatever *goal* a given YN happens to be asking whether the passage accomplished or not.

So after reading what the YN is asking about, you should likely trust what you think is the correct answer, read through the answer options, select what you think is correct, and move on.

The Next Level:

I always read every single answer option to every single question. The primary reason I do so is because I am trying to get all 75 English questions correct, and I know that I have no concern about finishing all of the questions smoothly within the standard time limit.

That said, I do think it is legitimate for students to not read all four answer options.

Upon reading what a YN is asking, I think it is very possible that you will be certain that you either need one of the "Yes" options or one of the "No" options. If this is the case, I think it is very much ok to carefully read only the two options that you think are possible to be correct, and then choose the one between them that you think is the best option.

2 *The A to D Question (AD)*

Potential Frequency:

It would seem like you can anticipate seeing this type of question on the day of your exam about two times.

Priority Level:

Similar to the YN that we just discussed, there is nothing heavy duty to know here, and this question type seems like it will be a staple to the test. Therefore, pick this one up my friend.

Fundamental Idea/Approach:

It will not be difficult to recognize this question when it appears. If it is present within a given English block, it will either be the final question in the block or the second to last question in the block. And the answer options will contain the four letters from A to D, hence why I chose to name this one what I did.

The idea of the question is to take a new line and fit it in to one of four possible spots within the original passage. It might take a practice question or two to get accustomed to smoothly seeing those four lettered spots within the passage, but each answer option does clearly indicate which paragraph each lettered option is located within. And each letter option will be set up in brackets, so it shouldn't take long for you to get used to seeking out the [A], [B], [C], and [D] that are parts of this question type.

So, also similar to the YN, there is a very good chance that you are already very well equipped to tackle this question head on. Since you were reading the passage and paying decent attention along the way while you were reading the passage, it is quite possible it will make natural sense to you where to add in the proposed line. If it is not clear to you where to add it, it is very likely that at the minimum, there are two locations that you can rule out.

Given what the proposed new line happens to be about, there are likely at least two proposed spots that simply seem silly to consider because the proposed line doesn't have much to do with the paragraph that two of the proposed spots are parts of. As long as you are not feeling artificially rushed through this question, at the worst, you should be able to take a strong 50-50 shot at any AD.

The Next Level:

If you do happen to find yourself between two options, or if you want to be a bit extra sure that you have located the proper spot to put the proposed sentence, you should definitely read at least the sentence before and after the bracketed-letter location.

It is definitely possible that a given proposed sentence could seem like it fits in a particular location because it seems to connect to the sentence that is before it. But if you were to read the sentence after it, you might realize that it actually would be a bit disjointed to put in that particular spot.

This circumstance will not likely be overly common. I do think that out of two potential ADs on a given test, at least one of the two will likely pose no threat to you. Once you locate all four lettered spots within the passage, it will likely be clear to you where to put the proposed sentence for at least one of the ADs that happen to be on a given test.

Depending on what dream you are trying to make a reality, bear down and get all ADs on a given exam or be somewhat ok with maybe running into one that is a touch less crystal clear.

Final Comment:

As you get deeper into this part of the book, and as you get more and more familiar with the various types of questions that exist within the English portion of the ACT, it is likely that you should make personal decisions regarding how you might want to allocate your time and energy on test day.

There is a very good chance that you will not feel pressured for time within the English portion of the test. But if you did, then at some point, you might need to make the decision to sacrifice one type of question for the greater good of making sure that you did another type of question very slowly and carefully.

If you do end up getting to that sort of necessary decision, it is likely that you should choose the ADs to be ones that you do attempt to do slowly, carefully, and therefore, accurately.

3. The Addition Question (AQ)

Potential Frequency:

It would seem like you can anticipate seeing this type of question on the day of your exam at least once, and quite possibly, two or three times.

Priority Level:

Now we start to venture into the pattern-recognition part of our question type journey. There are a couple of patterns to memorize here, and at the minimum, you need to memorize the first one. If you can memorize them both, that would be amazing!

Fundamental Idea/Approach:

When this question type pops up, it should likely be obvious, as the wording of the question is basically the same every time. That said, it could sort of seem like a hybrid of the first two question types that we have discussed, so if there is some initial confusion with identifying these AQs, that would be understandable.

That said, the typical AQ (like the AD) is giving you something new to consider *adding*. And then the four answer options are split between two "Yes" options and two "No" options. Let's now address classic correct answer type #1.

Over the years, a super common correct answer has been a "No" option that indicates that what is being considered to add is not necessary to add because it is basically *irrelevant*. So, when you encounter an AQ, if your first natural thought is that what is being considered to add is not really relevant to what you had been reading thus far, you are likely dealing with a very classic AQ.

You could potentially ignore the two "Yes" options and see which of the two "No" options properly captures the idea that what is being considered to add is not necessary. Definitely keep in mind there are many ways for a given "No" option to indicate the idea of irrelevancy.

The Next Level:

Now, let's talk about a classic correct "Yes" response.

A classic "Yes" option to consider choosing is one that indicates that what is being considered to add would provide *specific* new examples or details. If such a "Yes" was the correct option to select, I suspect that you will clearly recognize that what was being considered to add was definitely not irrelevant.

Final Comment:

If you are uncertain as to what to put for a given AQ, then historically more of them have been the "No" option. I am confident that you will likely be able to decide whether to "Yes" or "No" on test day.

A final thing to acknowledge is that other types of "No" and "Yes" options can be correct, but there is a very good chance that the AQs that you run into on any given test will conform to the classic answer options that have now been detailed.

4 *The Homophone Question (HQ)*

Potential Frequency:

It would seem like you can anticipate seeing this type of question on the day of your exam at least two times.

Priority Level:

Let's shift gears again. We were just talking about memorizing some established patterns on the exam. Now let's talk about memorizing some straight up facts. And given that you can likely memorize a lot some of the information that is about to follow, mastering this type of question to at least some degree is a must.

Fundamental Idea/Approach:

This question type will reveal itself very naturally as you will see answer options that have homophones. If you forgot that homophones are words that sound the same, but mean different things, well then, now you know again.

The basic idea to hopefully crushing this type of question is simply to memorize as much as you can within the Raw Content portion of this question type. I have put the homophones in alphabetical order. You will notice, though, that there are asterisks in front of some of the items. These items are massively important, because they are more likely to come up, so definitely at least learn those items. And, of course, it would be super cool if you ended up memorizing everything here.

Raw Content:

*affect / effect

"affect" is a VERB and "effect" is a NOUN

    Ex. I am going to *affect* your SAT score by providing you with this book.

    Ex. The *effects* of smoking are exceptionally harmful. Don't smoke stupid!

dual / duel

"dual" basically means two

    Ex. In college, Julia plans to take on a *dual* major of economics and political science.

A "duel" is a fight.

> Ex. I challenged a student to a *duel* after he insulted my love of all things Adidas.

fair / fare

A "fair" can be a festival, like the county fair. You can also obviously use the word as an adjective to indicate something is right or just.

"fare" typically deals with money

> Ex. The *fare* for my Uber ride was ridiculous due to surge pricing.

*its / it's / its'

The first "its" is to show SINGULAR POSSESSION.

> Ex. I love the Adidas shirt I am wearing, and *its* material is very soft.

The second "it's" is a CONTRACTION for 'it is'.

> Ex. I love it when *it's* about 73 degrees outside.

The third one is NOT a word! So I won't give you an example with *its'*, since there is no acceptable example to give. If you ever see that one on an actual test, you can simply feel a sense of pity for any dufus who actually ends up choosing it.

*than / then

Use "than" to make a COMPARISON. Use "then" in all other circumstances.

If there is a comparison being made, thereby requiring the use of *than*, it should likely be pretty clear.

> Ex. You are more likely to be crushed by a random rock *than* ever get attacked by a shark.

*their / there / they're

The first "their" is to show PLURAL POSSESSION.

> Ex. I love the Adidas shirts I own, and *their* material is very soft.

The second "there" you should simply know when to use. If you don't, *there* just might not be any hope that *there* is a college that you can go to.

The third "they're" is a CONTRACTION for 'they are'.

> Ex. Acai bowls are delicious, and *they're* also healthy for you.

5. *The Sentence Re-Arrangement Question (SR)*

Potential Frequency:

It would seem like you can anticipate seeing this type of question on the day of your exam at least once, and possibly, twice.

Priority Level:

A great test taker understands the importance of prioritizing and having a sense of what his individual dream might be. Accordingly, this type of question may be the one you dislike the most, and therefore, it can have the lowest priority. Or, you might be trying to pick up everything from LTSA, and if that is the case, then try to pick this one up as well.

Fundamental Idea/Approach:

Building off of what we were just talking about, let me now acknowledge that about at least half of the people who read this book should decide that they simply don't need to really care about this type of question.

SRs are likely the more time-consuming type of question, especially if you want to take a really good shot at it. The simple aspect of this type of question is recognizing it. The question mentions a specific sentence that is numbered within the passage. And the question asks you to consider moving that sentence to a new position within a given paragraph or to decide to leave it where it originally was placed.

So, who can afford to *choose* to basically ignore this question?

Actually, the happy news is that the answer is many, many students!

A student who hopes to score into the 30s could ignore this question type. Disregarding this type of questions and scoring into the 30s would be sort of contingent on mastering nearly everything else within the English portion of the test that we talk about. But as you may already understand, mastering nearly everything else within the English portion of the test is actually possible given how direct much of the information is.

So, the first approach for many students will indeed be to simply choose a random answer to this type of question and blissfully move on to the next question on the day of the exam.

The Next Level:

Are you still reading?

Ok, if so, I assume you want to know more about our acquaintance the SR.

Let's begin by acknowledging that a classic misstep for students who do choose to confront the SR is that they don't properly acknowledge which sentence is supposed to be potentially moving in the first place. The sentence that is before the boxed out number of the question is very likely NOT the sentence that is potentially moving. You need to locate the sentence that comes after the number in the brackets.

So if you are being asked to consider moving "Sentence 2", then you need to find the "2" in the brackets [2] that is somewhere within the passage. It is the sentence AFTER that [2] that you are potentially moving.

Ok, with that out of the way, let's acknowledge that the most reliable way (please note that I am not saying the only way) to determine the correct answer is to read the entire paragraph that contains the sentence that you are potentially moving. And to ensure that you select the correct answer, you may need to do this four separate times.

Given that the first option is basically always going to be to keep it *where it is now*, the first thing I would do is read the original paragraph and see if the sentence in question happens to already be snugly in place. It is certainly quite possible that there is no need to move the given sentence. However, if the sentence in question did not seem like it was in the right place, I would then put it in the spot that the next answer option is telling me to put it in, and again, read the whole paragraph.

If you are going to commit to doing the SR, then to be sure you have the correct answer, it is possible that you will have read a given paragraph four times. In the past, it has taken me upwards of about two minutes to answer a given SR. The potential time investment and the potential effort investment are simply not worth it to many students. So again, if you do end up choosing to sacrifice this type of question, there would be a sound rationale behind doing so.

Final Comment:

Before we move on to the next type of question, it is worth acknowledging that there is a bit of an in-between technique to the SR.

With practice, I certainly do think it is possible to attempt an SR by reading the original paragraph, and as you read it, you might realize where the sentence should go. Peering at the choices, if you see what you are looking for, you could select the proper location and not necessarily re-read the paragraph multiple times over.

And actually, a second sort of in-between technique would be to plan on reading the paragraph potentially four separate times. But as you are doing so, if you do feel that you may have stumbled upon the correct answer without going through all four choices, you could potentially stop and simply choose that option.

Wonderfully, no matter what route you end up taking with the SRs, your amazing future will not be made or broken by them.

6. *The NOT Question (NQ)*

Potential Frequency:

It would seem like you can anticipate seeing this type of question on the day of your exam typically at least once or twice.

Priority Level:

Nothing heavy duty to pick up here my friend, so definitely just flat out memorize what is about to come.

Fundamental Idea/Approach:

This question type is basically impossible to miss as the basis of the question is that there is a capitalized "NOT" within the question, hence the very simplistic name of this type.

The idea of the question runs counter to almost the entire rest of the test, as you are now being asked to determine which of the four given options does NOT make the sentence that is involved within the question something grammatically acceptable.

This change of gears throws some people off initially, since basically in every other question you are trying to make things grammatically correct. But once you are aware of this question type's existence, you should be in fine shape.

Your approach to the NQ can simply be to read through each listed option and listen for what sounds off. It does not appear that the ACT is trying to make it overly difficult to discover which answer is the one that is NOT grammatically acceptable. It would appear that the ACT is simply trying to make sure that you can occasionally shift gears, follow a specific instruction, and smoothly then revert back to trying to make the rest of the questions grammatically correct.

The Next Level:

A final thing to mention is that a great habit to get into is to circle or box out the "NOT" when you see it within any NQ you encounter on test day. This is definitely something that I have done when I have taken recent live exams.

The idea is that by boxing out the "NOT", you remind yourself you're dealing with this type of question. That simple reminder may be all that's necessary to make sure that you don't accidentally choose an option that just sounds correct, since that is precisely what you are NOT looking to do for these NQs.

7. The Transition Word/Phrase Question (TW)

Potential Frequency:

It would seem like you can anticipate seeing this type of question on the day of your exam typically once or twice.

Priority Level:

Depending on how comfortable you get with some of the other question types, feeling great about this one may not be a major priority. Some people don't find this type of question to be an issue, while others end up really not liking it. By the time you are ready to take your final ACT, you should have a clear sense of how you feel about these TWs, but for now, it is quite ok if it's not a clear top or bottom priority.

Fundamental Idea/Approach:

The basic idea behind this question is to see if you can determine which given transition word or phrase would be the best way to connect the two parts of a given sentence. Or you may need to determine which transition word or phrase would be the best way to go from one sentence to the next within a given passage.

Transition words and phrases are words such as "however", "for example", and "consequently" to give you a few examples in case it wasn't clear what we were talking about here. When you encounter a TW, it should likely be very clear, as all four answer options will include different transition words or phrases.

The fundamental approach is to *at least* read the full sentence that contains the underlined transition word/phrase. I stressed "at least" in the previous sentence, because it is certainly possible that to really get a sense of which answer option is correct, you will need to read more than just one sentence. You might need to read the sentence before the one that contains the underlined transition word/phrase to get a clear enough sense of which answer option really works best.

The Next Level:

Some transition words and phrases are typically much more commonly familiar to most people, such as the three examples mentioned previously.

A solid technique to consider following through with would be to evaluate the answer options that you are most familiar with first. The idea here is that if one of those options does seem correct, you potentially not need to concern yourself with transition words and phrases that are a bit less familiar/kind of odd.

For instance, I would have a bit of a tough time perfectly articulating when to use a transition phrase like "it might be said". To some students, that phrase might not even seem like a transition phrase, but it certainly is. It's just not one that basically anyone ever uses in real life.

So before you trouble yourself with whether such a phrase like "it might be said" is the correct answer option to select, maybe first consider more traditional options like "however".

Raw Content:

To ensure that you can best evaluate some of the more commonly recognizable transition words/phrases, let's just be safe now and go over the basics of what some of them mean/imply.

Here are the current essentials to be familiar with.

consequently - This is a cause & effect word. If it was correct, there should be a clear connection between what is stated before the word and what is stated after the word.

for example - Might seem silly to actually write this, but if this was the correct transition phrase, then what came after it should clearly be an example of what had just been stated.

however - This is a contrast word. If it was correct, what is stated before the word should clearly contrast with what comes after the word.

moreover - This might be the least familiar item listed here, but it has reared it's head on a good number of standardized test questions in the past. This word is what I refer to as a continuation transition word, as it should build off of what had just been previously stated. It basically works the same as the phrase "in addition".

> Ex. Soccer has an extremely loyal fan base, moreover, it is a beloved sport around the globe.

Final Comment:

So hopefully on the day of your test, if you run into a couple of TWs, both of them will end up having correct answers that are fairly common transition words/phrases. However, correct answers to TWs will most definitely not always be the more familiar ones.

Starting out by judging the more familiar ones is a very valid course of action. And if it turns out that none of those feel right to you, then you will hopefully feel comfortable choosing one of the less familiar answer options.

8. The Keep/Delete Question (KD)

Potential Frequency:

It would seem like you can anticipate seeing this type of question on the day of your exam at least once.

Priority Level:

This question type seems to conform to some patterns, so it is one that you should likely commit to learning. Also, given that the patterns that are about to be discussed are things that we have already talked about, it should be quite manageable to add this question type to your skill set.

Fundamental Idea/Approach:

The setup of this question will make it obvious when you encounter it. The four answer options will compel you to decide whether a given sentence should be "Kept" within the passage or "Deleted" from the passage. There will be two of each type of answer option.

Now getting right to the pattern side of things, it seems like this question is set to operate similar to the Addition Question that we already spoke about. If you need to make reference back to that question info, then definitely do so.

So on the real day of your exam, do not be surprised if you end up choosing a "Delete" option because the sentence that is being considered seems pretty much irrelevant to the passage that you are reading.

The Next Level:

Again, in keeping with our friend the AQ, this type of question will certainly not always be the same kind of answer.

It is certainly quite possible that you should be thinking that the sentence under consideration should be "Kept", especially because you think that the sentence is providing specific new details or examples that do nicely align with whatever is being discussed within the passage.

Final Comment:

Unlike the AQ, which seems to lean toward the "No" side of the answer spectrum, it does not appear that the KD has an inclination. So go into any KD without being predisposed to choosing either of the two major types of answer options.

9. The Divide the Paragraph Question (DP)

Potential Frequency:

It would seem like you can expect to see this type of question maybe once on the day of your exam.

Priority Level:

As we talk about from time to time, given that this is nothing heavy duty to pick up, you should just pick this one up my friend.

Fundamental Idea/Approach:

This will be a very simple question to spot, as it will have a somewhat bulky initial set-up, but right toward the beginning, it will flat out tell you that it wants you to *divide this paragraph*.

How the question wants you to split the paragraph into two separate paragraphs will also be very specifically noted within the question. So actually, as long as you read precisely what a given DP is asking you to do, it should be very likely that you should get just about any DP that you stumble upon.

The Next Level:

The one mildly tricky aspect of this question is tied to what a given DP states at the very end. Either the word "before" or "after" will be mentioned. And which of those two words is mentioned is definitely a very big deal.

Let's pretend that you know that the location that a given paragraph should be split, based on what a specific DP was stating for you to do, is between Sentence 4 and Sentence 5.

If the final statement in the DP asked you to begin the new paragraph AFTER a given sentence, then the answer would be Sentence 4 in this case. But if the final statement in the DP asked you to begin the new paragraph BEFORE a given sentence, then the answer would be Sentence 5.

A DP could use either word at the end, so don't let that potentially subtle difference sneak by you on test day.

10. The Vocab-ish Question (VQ)

Potential Frequency:

It would seem like you can anticipate seeing this type of question on the day of your exam about two times.

Priority Level:

From a strategy standpoint, this type of question has the LOWEST priority level.

It is quite simple why this is true: this type of question cannot really be prepared for.

Fundamental Idea/Approach:

The main thing I need you to know about this type of question is simply that it is coming. But again, there is basically nothing you can do to be more ready for it than you already are.

The classic VQ will give you four words or phrases that are all likely to be very different from each other. The idea is that one of them is simply the best word/phrase to use within the context of the given sentence/passage.

Because the words that will appear within a given VQ will vary from question to question, there really is no way to prepare for this type of question ahead of time. It is quite possible that all of the words will be words that you are very familiar with, but it is also possible that there may be a word or two that you don't really know well how to use in context.

What you will basically do is just read all four options within the given sentence and trust whatever you think is the best answer to select.

The Next Level:

There is one other thing that you can keep in mind, though this is far from a make or break idea.

If within the four options, there happens to be a word that you do not know, then the proper thing to do is leave it alone. Do NOT just cross it off because you don't know what it means.

What you would want to do is judge the words you do know first. If you feel confident that one of the words that you do know is the correct answer, then you are good to go, and then it would not have mattered what that unknown word meant.

On the other hand, if none of the words that you do know seem to really be right, it is possible that the correct answer is the word that you do not know. It is not very comfortable for many students to choose an answer option that contains a word that they do not know, but doing so could be the right decision for a given VQ.

All of that said, there is a very good chance that this circumstance does not even present itself on the day of your exam.

11. *The If-Delete Question (ID)*

Potential Frequency:

It would seem like you can anticipate seeing this type of question on the day of your exam potentially once or twice.

Priority Level:

This is not a high priority question, as similar to the VQ, a primary objective of us discussing it is simply so that you are aware of its existence. But as is a theme pretty much within the entirety of LTSA, if you can this to your skill set, then definitely do so my friend.

Fundamental Idea/Approach:

First off, this will not be a difficult question to recognize. It should begin with the word "If", and then shortly thereafter you should see the word "delete". The basic idea of the question is to ask you what would happen if a given part or parts were deleted from the original passage.

The basic approach to this kind of question is in line with what you should naturally be doing anyway. While you are reading each English passage, you definitely should be paying solid attention to what the passage itself is about. You are stopping along the way obviously to answer each question as it comes up. But as you are doing that, you should also be paying attention to what is happening within the passage. Doing so should likely naturally equip you to effectively handle this type of question.

That said, for a given ID, it is certainly possible that you should carefully reread the particular sentence that contains the item(s) that are being proposed to delete. Rereading a particular sentence could potentially make it even clearer what would happen if a given part of a given sentence was deleted.

So in summation, this is a type of question in which it is likely that your instinct is in primary control. Like I said earlier, similar to our discussion of the VQ, part of the importance of this discussion is to make you aware of the ID's existence.

The Next Level:

In case you were wondering, there does not seem to be any pattern that this question or its answer options seems to conform to.

So don't invoke any pattern or strategy from any other type of question or any other part of this portion of the book while tackling an ID.

The only other piece of advice that I would pass along is to simply read through each answer option slowly and carefully. It would be pretty easy to read through a given choice and slightly misinterpret what it might have stated. So stay steady, don't rush, and you'll likely smoothly knock out any ID you come across.

12 *The Add a Sentence Question (AS)*

Potential Frequency:

It would seem like you can anticipate seeing this type of question on the day of your exam just once, or actually, maybe not at all.

Priority Level:

Given that there is a chance that you won't even see an AS on test day, this is obviously not a high priority. But what's about to follow is pretty light material, so maybe for the sake of thoroughness or diligence, see if you can comfortably add this item to your skill set.

Fundamental Idea/Approach:

It should likely be pretty simple to identify an AS if you see one. This question might look a bit like an AQ or even an SR, but it is definitely its own thing.

An AS isn't asking whether you should or should not add a given sentence like an AQ does. An AS is telling you that you are going to add a given sentence, and the question is where to put it. The where to put it part might make it seem like a SR, but I think nearly every student will agree that this question type is much less of a hassle than the typical SR.

After you have read the sentence that the question is telling you that you need to add, you should just go right to the first location that you are being given to consider and check if slotting it into that spot seems to make the most logical sense. It will likely be clear when you have found the right location, because there will very likely be a very clear connection both toward the beginning of the sentence and the end of the sentence.

For instance, if it turns out that the correct answer is to put the new sentence after Sentence 2, then the end of Sentence 2 will almost definitely say something that is mentioned at the beginning of the added sentence. And then the end of the added sentence will also almost definitely say something that is at the beginning of Sentence 3. Basically, the sentence that we were being compelled to add should slot in perfectly between two sentences within the given paragraph and there will be clear clues, both at the beginning and the end of the added sentence, that should make it clear you have found the right location to add the sentence to.

The Next Level:

If the correct location to add the new sentence happens to be *before Sentence 1*, then two things will likely be true. The beginning of the added sentence will likely sound like a good introduction. And then the end of the added sentence should definitely mention something that connects smoothly with what had previously been the first sentence of the paragraph.

Somewhat similarly, if the correct location to add the new sentence happens to be after the final sentence in the given paragraph, then the final sentence of the existing paragraph should definitely end with something that clearly connects to the beginning of the added sentence.

To sum up, if the added sentence ends up going first or last within the given paragraph, then there should only be one connection, versus when the added sentence ends up between two existing sentences, which should mean there are two clear connections.

Final Comment:

If what has been stated thus far about AS questions is not crystal clear, seeing even one example in practice should likely clarify things. And when it's all said and done, this is the second-to-last question type being mentioned for a reason: if there's only one of these on the day of your exam, then this is clearly not the linchpin of your overall English score.

13 *The Other Instructions Question (OI)*

Potential Frequency:

Because this last category is a bit of a catch-all, the frequency will vary from test to test, but expect to see a good number of these items on the day of your real exam.

Priority Level:

These questions must be given some degree of importance both because there could be quite a few of them that fall into this category on test day and because from a strategy standpoint, there is nothing crazy that you need to learn.

Fundamental Idea/Approach:

How you will identify an OI may be so simplistic that it may be a mild challenge at first.

OIs will have instructions after the question number, but those instructions will not be ones that we have already categorized. To hopefully make that comment crystal clear, let's acknowledge that the very first type of question that we discussed within this part of the book, the YN, also has instructions. The last two question types that we just spoke about prior to having this discussion, the ID and the AS, also have instructions.

The difference is that every other type of question that has instructions that we have given names to have very exact instructions, instructions that are worded the same way on basically every test. This is why those questions were given their own names and fall into distinct categories.

The OI category is for all of the "others". The questions that have instructions, but these instructions are not ones that come up consistently or that have any specific strategy tied to them. And that is why the basic approach to OIs is to simply do what you are being told to do!

So if a question asks you to add something that is *relevant* to the rest paragraph that you are reading, then that's what you need to do.

To not oversimplify things too much, let's acknowledge that in order to know what would be the "relevant" thing to add, you would need to be paying solid attention to what the overall passage that you are reading is about. And you would potentially need to read a line or two after whatever is underlined that is tied to the OI that you happened to be dealing with. Happily, given that the English passages that we get on test day are nothing heavy duty, you should likely find it to be quite manageable to do these things.

Ok, before we go into a bit more detail, it is very important to establish now that our dear friend, English Mantra #1: *Shorter is Better* is NOT something that you should be thinking about during OIs. A shorter answer could be right for a given OI. A very, very long answer could be the right option for a given OI. The length of the answer does not matter when we are dealing with OIs. What matters is that you are doing what the instructions are commanding you to do.

The Next Level:

Ok, now it makes sense to reiterate that you're really going to simply need to react to what is put in front of you on a given exam, and that you should anticipate a potentially wide range of situations.

You will very potentially be able to deal with each situation quite comfortably, as long as you don't rush through reading the instructions and don't rush through reading the accompanying answer options.

To give you a second example, a different OI could ask you to *most effectively* lead into a given paragraph. In a case like this, it should make sense that you'd basically have to at least read two or three sentences into the paragraph that you are supposed to be leading into to determine which answer option is the correct one to select. Happily, there is a very good chance that as long as you do pay attention to a given OI's instructions and then follow what they are telling you to do that the correct answer will very naturally reveal itself.

Final Comment:

The wording of an OI could be very important, and sometimes there is something very subtle within the wording of a given question or within one of the answer options.

For example, if the word "procedures" was used, the fact that that word is PLURAL could matter. This may seem crazy nitpicky, but if you thought that only one thing was mentioned, then a plural word would make a given answer option incorrect.

And so, as we close out the last of our English specialty questions, let's acknowledge that for OIs, there really is nothing factual to memorize ahead of time to be ready for them. But to get as many of them correct as possible (which hopefully even means all of them!), you will need to potentially be very vigilant with the exact wording that happens to get used within a given question.

And if a given question feels a bit too cumbersome or awful, it is a strategically sound idea to let it go. Don't allow yourself to get stuck on it, and acknowledge that the right tactical decision is likely to trust whatever you think might be right and move on.

Three English Meditations

Before we leave the realm of English, let's address some final key ideas to make sure your mind is right on test day.

1. A Monster Start

I think it's a really great thing that the ACT starts with English. The English portion of the ACT is arguably the most preparable section of any standardized test that currently exists. This is simply because the English portion of the test consistently hits us with the same styles of questions, the same grammatical facts, and the same patterns within certain questions.

So basically, all I wanted to say here is that you can absolutely ensure that you get off to a monster start on test day. Know the material laid out within this part of the book to the highest degree possible. No matter what you are eventually hoping to have your Composite score be, an incredible foundation can be put into place when you crush this part of the exam.

2. Warm Up Your Brain

Building a bit off of the previous meditation, since we know how crushable the English part of the test is. And since we know that it will be the very first thing that we will face on the morning of the test. It is definitely a very, very good idea to warm your brain up a bit on the morning of the test.

This is nothing heavy duty. And what we are talking about here is definitely NOT trying to cram in some final facts or patterns on the morning of the exam. The idea is simply to read through some early part of the English chapter of this book for even just a few minutes. Maybe do this while you are eating breakfast. Or do this after you have arrived early at the school at which you are testing.

Given the early start of the ACT, and given that you are not typically accustomed to doing heavy duty academic work at like eight in the morning on a typical day, it would be smart if the very first thing that you saw on the day of your real exam isn't the actual test itself. By just reading back through a few key pages of your LTSA, you should find your brain now warmed up a bit and ready to attack the real exam.

3. One Time Check

As you'll see as you continue through the book, we won't talk much about time management and the clock. The reason why is because I know that if you cultivate all of the skills that you personally need to, you won't really need to be very aware of what your timing is like. That said, on the day of your exam, for certain sections, it does make sense to check the clock once, and so now let's elaborate on that thought.

If you aren't already very aware of it, the English section will have 75 total questions. The questions are split between five passages, and usually each passage contains 15 questions.

The standard time limit for the English section is 45 minutes. Now dividing that by five, since there are five passages, yields 9. This is our point of reference for the following categories.

▶ Under 6

If this is the time frame you notice that you are in after completing the first block of questions, you are considerably ahead of the clock. It would be advisable to consider consciously choosing to slow down a bit. Read through some of the upcoming questions a bit more slowly and carefully. And just about any question that you want to take your time with, you should be able to do so.

▶ 7 or 8

If you're within this time frame, things are moving at a very natural pace. Odds are you should just keep doing what you're doing. And you should be able to essentially ignore the clock for the rest of the section.

▶ 9 or more

You are behind the clock if you find yourself within this time frame. You should likely make the tactical decision to simply guess on a more cumbersome style of question like the SR for instance. Doing so should allow you to get to the final few questions without feeling rushed, which is definitely important given that there could be some very manageable questions toward the very end of the section.

Targets & Expectations

We will conclude each of the four main segments of this book with a discussion of targets and expectations. What is about to follow is meant to help you strike an appropriate balance between pushing yourself to reach your full potential and recognizing when maybe you've done what you needed to and it's time to move on from the wonderful world of the ACT.

▶ *34 or higher*

If you intend to be a hardcore ACT badass, then this is a part of the test in which you need to prove it. If you acquired nearly everything within this part of the book at some point within your preparation, you would end up with an English score in this range.

As previously stated, the English section of the ACT really does seem to be the most preparable aspect of any standardized test out there. So much repetitively appears exam after exam. So many facts and patterns are staples to the exam. Whether English was a natural strength or not, you could cultivate a very keen awareness of what you will encounter within this part of the test on the day of your real exam.

If your ultimate goal is to have a Composite score of 30 or higher, then hitting this range for this part of the test is basically a must.

▶ *Breaking 30*

I really believe that basically every student could break into the 30s in this part of the test. I don't think everyone can score as high as 34+, because doing so requires exceptionally high levels of motivation and determination, that quite frankly, most of us don't need to possess in order to make all sorts of exciting dreams come true.

But I do really believe that you can break into the 30s my friend. Doing so requires you to know a lot of what is within this part of the book, but that is possible. And happily, breaking 30 does leave you some room for error. There are types of questions that you don't ever need to get comfortable with, and there are concepts that you can afford not to understand.

And keep in mind that if you can break 30 within English, you may be giving yourself even more breathing room somewhere else along the way with this exam. If you don't love Math, get great at English. If you don't love Reading, get great at English. If you don't love Science, get great at English. Or maybe, just get great at English because you can.

▶ *Between 25 and 29*

This is the only other category I am listing here, because plain and simple, I know that at the least you can score within this range.

Memorize the Mantras soon. Then get a good handle on what is mentioned within the punctuation part of the book. Then start to memorize everything that you "MUST" memorize. Then pick up at least some of what is within the part of what you "SHOULD TRY" to memorize.

Sprinkle in some test seasoning from having sat for the real exam once or twice, and before you know it, you are comfortably scoring in the mid to high 20s. You don't need to be a naturally good test taker; the vast majority of us are not. You simply needed to be told what to actually know for an exam like the ACT. Consider yourself told my friend.

Math

Three Mantras

1) Skip Around

Math questions on standardized tests like the ACT were NOT meant to be done in order.

Particularly, as you get past a certain point within the 60-question Math section, it will become an essential tactical skill to appropriately and assertively skip around. It should make sense that within a set of 60 questions, it is basically impossible to establish a clear order of difficulty within the set. For instance, the writers of the ACT cannot perfectly ensure that question #50 is definitely more difficult than #40 for all students. What ultimately makes a question more or less difficult is simply whether you are familiar with the question.

So on test day, be as decisive as possible as you attack the questions, and don't allow yourself to get stuck on any given question. Skipping a question for any reason is a good reason, especially because skipping a question doesn't mean you have given up on the question. It just means that you don't want to get caught up on the question, and, of course, you can always attempt it later.

2) Don't Skip Steps

The most surefire way to avoid making minor mistakes on test day is to literally show every step as you solve any given question.

$$\text{Ex.} \quad 3x + 8 = 4$$

It is so easy to see what is above and make a quick mental mistake. Before you know it, you have written down $3x = 12$, and you are on the road to a classic error.

If you *chose* to simply write down "-8" and "-8" on both sides of the equation, you would end up with proper result of $3x = -4$

To ensure that you avoid making classic minor mistakes, don't skip steps!

③ Be Flexible

Tests like the ACT give us options. Taking full advantage of those options is the mark of a master test taker.

As you will soon read, there are several ways to tackle Math questions that go outside the boundaries of traditional mathematics.

Ultimately, it doesn't matter how you end up with a correct answer, as long as what you did is legitimate.

Let's see just what it means to be flexible.

Four Alternatives to Standard Math

Have you caught on yet to the idea of what we are really trying to do?

During the English portion of this book, my goal was not to make you a better writer, or to help you speak English more properly, or to make you smarter in general. My goal was simple: get you ready for the specific things that you need to know that tie particularly to the ACT.

Along those lines, I now need to clue you in to an important secret that really shouldn't be a secret to anyone. Because if you think that all there is to mastering the Math portion of the ACT is knowing a lot of mathematics, then my friend, you don't know what tests like the ACT really allow us to do.

Let's make some more dreams turn into realities!

① *Use the Given Answers (UGA)*

Sometimes the best thing to do is simply use the answers that are provided and just see which one actually works. This is a classic technique that has been available for students to take advantage of since the dawn of standardized tests.

When you use this technique, it makes sense to start by testing the middle option, which will either be option (C) or (H). The idea is that if the first option you try is too big or too small, you would conceivably know how to adjust and then you wouldn't need to try all five options to find the correct answer.

On any given exam, it would be quite possible that you could employ UGA *at least* 3-5 times scattered throughout the Math section.

② *Draw Your Own Diagram (DOD)*

If a question dealing with geometry or coordinate geometry does not provide you with a diagram, it is quite possible that drawing your own diagram could help you arrive at the correct answer.

If you are going to draw your own diagram, take the time to draw it well. The better your diagram, the more likely it is that a correct answer could reveal itself quite naturally.

③ Substitute Your Own Numbers (SYON)

All standardized tests that include a Math section eventually allow you to take advantage of this classic test-taking technique.

For some questions, the best thing to do is just to choose your own number for a given variable or some other unknown within the question. Using that number, you can see what would happen very concretely.

It may seem surprising that it would be ok to essentially just choose a random number to solve a given question, but very simply, this is something that certain multiple choice questions allow us to do. That said, to ensure that there nothing quirky happens on test day, do NOT use 0 or 1 as your random number. These two numbers are very special in mathematics. Using either one could cause a coincidence that could lead to a mistake on test day.

④ Trial & Error (TE)

You may not use this technique much on the day of your test, but for the sake of thoroughness, I need to include it here. Because even if it gives you one extra question, that's an extra question that could just be that final piece of the puzzle to swing your score to what you are hoping it will be.

The idea here is simple: pick a somewhat random value to potentially be the correct answer to a given question. Assuming your first selection doesn't lead you directly to the correct answer, you will keep trying other trials until you find the one that does.

This may seem like a potentially time-consuming process, but usually, it actually really isn't. There will only be one trial that makes everything within the question work, and once you find it, it should be 100% clear that you have found it.

Things You MUST Memorize

1 The AREA of a CIRCLE is pi times the radius squared.

2 The CIRCUMFERENCE of a CIRCLE is two times pi times the radius.

3 The AREA of a TRIANGLE is one-half times the base times the height.

And keep in mind that the *height* of a triangle is always the straight up and down distance from the top of the triangle to the base of the triangle.

4 The PERIMETER of any shape is all of the sides added together.

5 The AREA of a PARALLELOGRAM is just base times height.

Just like with a triangle, you must keep in mind that the *height* of a parallelogram is always the straight up and down distance from the top of the parallelogram to the bottom. And if you forgot what a parallelogram is, think of it as a slanted rectangle.

6 There are 180 degrees within a triangle.

So if you knew two angles within a given triangle, you could certainly determine the third angle by subtracting the other two values from 180.

7 The VOLUME of a rectangular box is length times width times height.

8 Angles that are directly next to each other on a straight line must add up to 180 degrees.

So if you had two angles sitting side by side on a straight line, and you knew the value of one of the two angles, you could get the other angle by subtracting the known value from 180.

9 There are 360 degrees in a circle.

10 The ORIGIN is another way of saying the coordinates (0,0) on a typical xy-coordinate graph.

11 **The Pythagorean Theorem is something that you only use with RIGHT TRIANGLES.**

The Pythagorean Theorem is traditionally articulated as a-squared plus b-squared equals c-squared. [$a^2 + b^2 = c^2$] Keep in mind that the letters used don't really matter as long as you know where to actually put any given values.

The key thing is that the longest side (the hypotenuse) is always on one side of the equation by itself and that the other two smaller sides are together on the other side of the equation. So, if you know any two sides of a given right triangle, you can use the Pythagorean Theorem to determine the missing third side.

12 **All four-sided shapes (quadrilaterals) have interior angles that add up to a total of 360 degrees.**

13 **First imagine that you were given a standard function such as $f(x) = 3 - 5x$**

Now, if you were asked something like f(-3), all you are being asked to do is put the value in the parentheses, in this case the -3, in for 'x' in the original function.

So, f(-3) would equal 3 - 5(-3), which would end up equaling 18.

14 **A classic algebra mistake is not properly distributing a negative sign.**

　　　　Ex.　　13x - (5 - 2x)

Running through something like this too quickly, it would be very easy to forget to have the negative that is in front of the parentheses affect the '-2x'.

In this case, properly distributing the negative means you would end up with the following.

　　　　Ex.　　13x - (5 - 2x)　—>　13x - 5 + 2x

15 **If you forgot how to FOIL, then it's time to bring it back into your active skill set.**

FOIL stands for First, Outside, Inside, Last.

　　　　Ex.　　(2x - 5) (x + 6)

FIRST , you would multiply the '2x' and 'x' to get $2x^2$.

Then you would go OUTSIDE and multiply the '2x' and '6' to get 12x.

Now go INSIDE and multiply the '-5' and 'x' to get -5x.

Finally, multiply the LAST items of '-5' and '6' to get -30.

After you combine the like terms, you should have a final result of $2x^2 + 7x - 30$

16 **To compute a standard percentage, you should first convert a given percentage into a decimal. To do so, you can put a decimal point after the percentage number, and then move it to the left two places.**

    Ex.   7% —> .07

Then to compute the percentage, multiply that decimal by whatever number you were trying to get the percentage of.

    Ex.   42% of 58 —> .42 x 58

17 **A classic time to set up a proportion would be when you are given three values and you are being asked to determine a fourth value.**

    Ex.   If 18 cups of flour make 4 cookies, then how many cups of flour would be necessary to make 10 cookies.

In this case, you can set up the following proportion: $18 / 4 = x / 10$

When you set up the proportion, be sure to put items that are the same in the same position. So in this case, I put both of the "cookies" numbers on the bottoms of the two fractions.

To solve a standard proportion, you CROSS-MULTIPLY.

So in this case, you would end up getting $4x = 180$. Then dividing both sides by 4, you would end up with a final result of 45.

18 **The SLOPE-INTERCEPT form of a line has a set appearance, one in which the "y" is all by itself.**

    Ex. $y = -4x + 7$

In this format, the number by itself represents the Y-INTERCEPT, which is where the graph hits the y-axis.

The -4 that is in front of the 'x' represents the SLOPE.

If you were given the equation of a line that did not have "y" by itself, it would only be a matter of executing a few steps to put such an equation into slope-intercept form.

    Ex. $10x + 3y = 5$

If you subtracted '10x' from both sides to move that item over, you would now have $3y = -10x + 5$.

From here, you could divide both sides by '3', which would yield an equation with "y" now by itself, $y = -10/3x + 5/3$.

Interpreting this equation, we could say the slope was -10/3 and the y-intercept is 5/3.

19 **Given how long it has likely been since you have had to solve some fundamental equations, it wouldn't be strange if you had to brush up some of your old skills.**

   Ex. $3(x - 2) + 5(x + 2) = 10x$

Take your time to properly distribute both sets of parentheses.

   Ex. $3x - 6 + 5x + 10 = 10x$

A classic mistake is to forget to multiply one of the items within the parentheses by the number that was outside of the parentheses. Dodging that minor potential error, you can now combine your like terms.

   Ex. $8x + 4 = 10x$

From there, don't rush any of the final steps. Subtracting '8x' from both sides will yield $4 = 2x$ and then it is only a matter of dividing both sides by 2 to yield a final results of $x = 2$.

20 **There are separate relationships between lines and their slopes when lines are either *parallel* or *perpendicular*.**

When lines are PARALLEL, they have the same slope.

When lines are PERPENDICULAR, their slopes are opposite reciprocals.

   Ex. $y = -3x + 6$

Within this example, a *parallel* line to the line in the example would also have a slope of -3.

And within the same example, a *perpendicular* line to the line in the example would have a slope of 1/3.

21 **A classic algebra maneuver is to *multiply both sides by the denominator* to get rid of a fraction.**

   Ex. $5/2x = 11$

In this case, if you multiplied both sides by '2x', which is the denominator of the given fraction, you would end up with $5 = 22x$.

From there, you could divide both sides by 22 to get a final result for 'x' of 5/22.

There are quite a few circumstances in which multiplying by a given denominator makes it easier to move forward within a given question. And this is a move that does not really depend on whatever the denominator happens to be.

22) Let's review how to solve a standard quadratic that can be factored.

In such a situation, the given quadratic must be set equal to 0, so if it is not already, then you need to move whatever items you need to move so that the quadratic is set equal to 0.

   Ex. $x^2 - 30 = x$

Subtracting 'x' from both sides, we would then end up with a quadratic set equal to 0.

   Ex. $x^2 - x - 30 = 0$

Now you would need to remember how to factor to arrive at $(x - 6)(x + 5) = 0$

Core factoring requires the two numbers that you end up with to MULTIPLY to equal the number that was originally by itself. So in this case, -6 multiplied by 5 would yield -30.

Core factoring also requires the two numbers that you end up with to ADD up to the number that is front of the 'x' term. So in this case, -6 and 5 added together would yield the -1 that we can imagine is in front of the 'x'.

From here, remember that the solutions would be the opposites of the values in the parentheses, because you are technically setting each set of parentheses equal to 0.

So in this case, '6' and '-5' would be the final solutions.

23) Four fundamental statistical terms are *mean, median, mode,* and *range*.

The *mean* is just another way to say AVERAGE.

The *median* is the MIDDLE value when the values have been arranged in order.

The *mode* is the value that appears MOST frequently.

And the *range* is the DIFFERENCE between the largest and smallest values.

24 **You can get the MIDPOINT of two points by doing AVERAGE.**

For example, imagine you were told that one point on a coordinate graph was (-1,5) and another point was (5,11).

The x-coordinate of the midpoint would be the average of -1 and 5, which would be 2, since adding -1 and 5 gives you 4 and dividing that by 2 gives you 2.

The y-coordinate of the midpoint would be the average of 5 and 11, which would be 8, since adding 5 and 11 gives you 16 and dividing that by 2 gives you 8.

25 **Remember that when you are calculating an ABSOLUTE VALUE expression, you always do the actual calculation first.**

For example, if you had | 3 - 8 | , the first thing you would do is the 3 minus 8, which would yield -5.

After the computation was done, now you would switch the negative result to a positive value, leaving us in this case with a final result of positive 5.

And remember that absolute value brackets only change negative results to positive results. Any positive result stays positive.

26 **If you are trying to use your calculator to do a trigonometric calculation, for instance, something with *sin* or *cos*, and PI is involved, then your calculator needs to be in RADIAN (RAD) mode.**

If you don't currently know how to switch your calculator from DEGREE (DEG) mode to RAD mode, then you should probably figure that out prior to test day!

Things You Should TRY to Memorize

1 **The AREA of a TRAPEZOID is one half times the sum of the two bases times the height. [A = 1/2(Base 1 + Base 2) h]**

2 **The VOLUME of a CYLINDER is pi times the radius squared times the height.**

3 **There are two very classic ways to shift the graph of a normal function.**

     A) If you added/subtracted a value to the function OUTSIDE of the parentheses.

     Ex.   If you were given f(x) and then you were given f(x) - 5

In this case, the graph of the function would go DOWN 5. If a number had been *added* instead of subtracted, the graph would have moved UP.

     B) If you added/subtracted a value to the function INSIDE of the parentheses.

     Ex.   If you were given f(x) and then you were given f(x - 5)

In this case, the graph of the function would go RIGHT 5. If a number had been *added* instead of subtracted, the graph would have moved LEFT.

Moving left and right is opposite to your natural instinct, as a negative should typically make you think left and a positive should typically make you think right. But horizontal moves are, like I said, the opposite of your natural instinct.

4 **PRIME numbers are numbers that can only be divided by themselves and 1.**

The first prime number is 2. Other examples of prime numbers are 3, 5, 7, 11, and 13. The number 2 is also the only prime number that is even, since all other even numbers can be divided by 2.

5. Here are three classic situations involving exponents.

A) $(x^4)(x^3) \rightarrow x^7$

Remember that when you are multiplying two different terms with the same base, you ADD the exponents.

B) $(x^8)/(x^2) \rightarrow x^6$

Now also remember that when you are dividing two different terms with the same base, you SUBTRACT the exponents.

C) $(x^4)^3 \rightarrow x^{12}$

When you raise a term with an exponent to another exponent, you MULTIPLY the exponents.

As a final thing to mention keep in mind that any numbers that are in front terms with exponents follow their own rules that are separate from what needs to happen with the terms with the exponents.

Ex. $(3x^2)(5x^3) \rightarrow 15x^5$

The exponents need to get added together, since this falls into the first situation described above in which two separate terms with the same base are being multiplied together. But the numbers in front are just normal numbers, so those numbers do need to get multiplied, which is why the end result has the '15' in front. This is a situation in which it is fairly easy to make a minor mistake, so if you see it on test day, take your time and carefully think through what you're seeing.

6. When there are PARALLEL LINES, certain angles will end up equaling each other.

A very reliable way to determine which angles equal each other is to think that angles that are on opposite sides of things end up being the ones that are equal. This is why there are formal geometry terms like 'alternate interior' and 'alternate exterior' when describing certain equal angles created by parallel lines.

7 **The LEAST COMMON DENOMINATOR (LCD) is the smallest number that different denominators all divide into evenly.**

For example, if you had the fractions 1/3, 2/5, and 5/6, the LCD would be 30, since 30 is the smallest number that the three different denominators of 3, 5, and 6 all divide into evenly.

8 **If you know the *solutions* of a given function or equation, then you can determine the *factors* of that function by remembering to switch the sign and by remembering how to properly write a factor.**

For example, if '5' was the *solution* of a given function, then (x - 5) would be a factor.

In another example, if '-3' was a solution, then (x + 3) would be a factor.

And keep in mind that this goes both ways. So if you were given the factors of a given function, you could then get the solutions (which could also be referred to as the *roots* or the *zeroes*).

So if I knew that (x - 4) was a factor, then '4' would be a solution.

9 **Every so often the ACT may give you a formula that it doesn't expect you to have memorized, and your job is just to use it.**

For example, you would not be expected to know the formula for the volume of a cone. But the ACT might give you a question in which it gives you the formula for the volume of a cone, and you simply need to put the right numbers into the right locations within the equation and calculate.

10 **A key move in a question involving a RATIO can be to add up the numbers in the ratio.**

A ratio represents different parts. By adding up the numbers in a given ration, you are determining the total number of parts involved in a given mathematical scenario.

    Ex.   The ratio of red to blue to yellow marbles is 3:2:4.

Adding up the numbers in the example, we can determine that in this situation, there is a total of 9 parts. Now, if we were told that there were 63 total marbles, we could determine the number of marbles for each color.

Dividing 63 by 9 (the total number of parts), we can determine that each part represents 7 marbles. Since the ratio indicates that "red" is 3 parts within the ratio, we now know that there are 21 (3 x 7) red marbles. We could then determine that there are 14 (2 x 7) blue marbles. And lastly, we could determine that there are 28 (4 x 7) yellow marbles.

⑪ Let's talk about SohCahToa.

First, this is a trigonometry concept that is only relevant when there is a *right triangle*. Now let's break down the parts.

      Soh —> sin = oppositie / hypotenuse

      Cah —> cos = adjacent / hypotenuse

      Tan —> tan = opposite / adjacent

When using SohCahToa it is super important to pay attention to which angle is being referenced in any given situation.

For example, let's imagine that we were given a right triangle labeled as ABC, with side AB as 8, side BC as 15, and side AC as 17.

If we were asked for "sin C", then we would need to first determine what is the "opposite" in this situation, since 'sin' is opposite over the hypotenuse. The "opposite" of angle C would be side AB, which is 8.

The typical simple part of SohCahToa is determining the hypotenuse as the hypotenuse doesn't depend on which angle we are referring to. So in this case, the hypotenuse, which is always the longest side, is 17.

Putting this together, we can say that "sin C" is equal to 8/17.

To try to cement this idea, let's now determine "tan A" with this same setup. Let's start by determining the "opposite" of angle A, which is going to be side BC, which is 15. Now that we have determined the "opposite", the side that is considered the "adjacent" is the other side that is not the hypotenuse, which in this case would be side AB, which is 8. Therefore, "tan A" is equal to 15/8.

For many students, the easiest way to determine which side is considered the "adjacent" is by first determining which side is the "opposite". The "adjacent" will always be the side that is both not the "opposite" and not the hypotenuse.

⑫ Now let's talk about the LAW of SINES.

Some people actually find this simpler to work with than SohCahToa, so if you didn't love the last discussion point, maybe pick this item up instead. Keep in mind we are in the part of the book in which you are *trying* to memorize certain key material. To make some of your dreams come true, you can likely afford to sacrifice an item or two within this part of the book.

The law of sines states that the sin of any angle over the side across from it is equal to the sin of any other angle over the side across from it.

To give you an example, let's imagine we have a triangle with angles of 110, 40, and 30. Now let's say that we knew that the length of the side across from the 110-degree angle was 12. We could now determine the lengths of the other two sides.

We could get the length of the side across from the 40-degree angle by setting up a proportion: sin 110 / 12 = sin 40 / x .

In this situation, by the way, the typical ACT question is not going to actually ask you to get an exact numeric value for 'x'. The question will likely want you to move things around so that 'x' is simply by itself.

In this case, we could cross-multiply to get x(sin 110) = 12 sin 40. Then we could divide both sides by sin 110, leaving us with a final result of x = 12 sin 40 / sin 110.

The last comment to make is that the law of sines can be used with any type of triangle, versus SohCahToa, which only is valid to use with right triangles.

13 If you were given the equation of a circle, you could determine two things from the equation: the circle's center and the circle's radius.

>   Ex. $(x + 2)^2 + (y - 4)^2 = 49$

The *center* will have the OPPOSITE signs of the numbers that are within the parentheses. So in this case, the center would be (-2,4).

The *radius* is always the SQUARE ROOT of the number that the equation is set equal to. So in this case, the radius would be 7.

14 If you are given a table or a bar graph that shows the frequency of given data, a key first step is likely to transcribe the table.

So imagine you were given a bar graph that showed how many siblings 20 different people polled stated they had. Let's imagine that the table indicated that 5 people stated that they had 0 siblings, 6 people stated that they had 1 sibling, and 9 people stated that they had 2 siblings.

To determine a variety of things, a key step would potentially be to write down five "0"s, followed by six "1"s, followed by nine "2"s. Now, for instance, if you were asked to find the average of all 20 people, you could add up all of the numbers that you wrote down and then divide by 20. Seeing all of the values written out, you could also very comfortably determine the median of the data set.

15 **If every term in an algebraic expression had the same variable, a potential first move would be to factor out that variable.**

Ex. $3x^3 - 2x^2 + 11x \longrightarrow x(3x^2 - 2x + 11)$

As you can see in the example above, an 'x' was taken out of each term.

What you would do from here would depend on the specific question. One firm statement that could be made (building a bit off of a previous idea) is that one *solution* within this expression is 0. If a variable, such as 'x', is by itself in such an expression, it simply means that 0 a solution.

16 **There are two special triangles that are distinguished by their angle measurements, the 30-60-90 and the 45-45-90.**

The 45-45-90 is typically the simpler of the two situations to memorize, as you only have two types of sides. There are the two equal sides (since there are two equal angles), and then there is the hypotenuse.

If you know one of the two equal sides, you would multiply by radical 2 to get the hypotenuse. Conversely, if you knew the hypotenuse, you would divide by radical 2 to get either of the two equal sides, also traditionally known as the legs.

Memorizing what's going on with the 30-60-90 is a touch more complicated.

If you were given the shortest side (which is the one opposite to the 30-degree angle), you could get the longer leg by multiplying by radical 3. And then you could also get the hypotenuse by doubling the shortest side.

If you were given the longer leg (which is the one opposite to the 60-degree angle), you would divide by radical 3 to get the shortest side. You could then double that value to get the hypotenuse.

17 **A *vertical asymptote* exists when the denominator of a fraction equals 0.**

So to determine a vertical asymptote(s), you can flat out set the denominator of a given fraction equal to 0.

Or, depending on the question, you could potentially implement Math Alternative #1: *Use the Given Answers* to see which number(s) will make the denominator equal to zero.

18 **ADDING or SUBTRACTING matrices is nothing heavy duty. You really will just add across or subtract across as your instincts likely may have told you to do.**

So if you were adding two matrices together, then whatever number is in the upper lefthand corner of one matrix will be added to whatever number is in the upper lefthand corner of the other matrix and that sum will be what you put in the upper lefthand corner of the correct answer.

19 **To *bisect* means to cut in HALF.**

20 **Let's discuss three classic types of triangles: equilateral, isosceles, and scalene.**

An *equilateral* triangle is one with three equal sides and all three angles must be 60 degrees.

An *isosceles* triangle is one with two equal sides, and because it has two equal sides, it must also have two equal angles.

A *scalene* triangle is any triangle with three different sides, and therefore, it also has three different angles.

21 **The REMAINDER is the *whole* number left over after you divide.**

To determine the remainder, most people should do any necessary work by hand and NOT with a calculator.

As an example, the remainder when you divide 13 by 4 is 1, since 4 goes into 13 three times and four time three would be 12, which would leave 1 left over from the original 13 that we were dividing into.

If you fired 13 divided by 4 into a calculator, you would get 3.25, which does not properly reveal the remainder.

22 A *solution set* is a single value within a bracket or multiple values within a bracket that represent ALL of the possible solutions for a particular situation.

      Ex. $x^2 - 3x - 10 = 0$ $\{-2, 5\}$

The solution set for the fairly straightforward quadratic above is made up of the two values that are within the brackets.

A solution set shows all individual values that make a given situation true or equal.

      Ex. $\{-1, 0, 4, 11\}$

This solution set would mean that each of the four values within the brackets would separately make the given situation true or equal.

23 If you were given equations of lines that only had an 'x' or only had a 'y', you would be dealing with vertical and horizontal lines.

When there is only an 'x', you are dealing with a VERTICAL LINE.

      Ex. $x = 5$ This is a vertical line that you would draw where 'x' is 5.

When there is only a 'y', you are dealing with a HORIZONTAL LINE.

      Ex. $y = -2$ This is a horizontal line that you would draw down where 'y' is -2.

This idea is a bit opposite to what your natural instinct should likely be saying to you, so just be a touch careful not to flip things in your head.

Things You CHOOSE to Memorize

1 **Let's start this block with the *difference of two squares*, also possibly known as DOTS if you were taught that acronym.**

>   Ex. $x^2 - 49$

An item like what is above can be factored to $(x + 7)(x - 7)$.

The idea is very exact. First you will always end up with two sets of parentheses, one of which has a "+" sign and the other of which has a "-" sign.

What will go in the parentheses will always be the square root of the original items, whether those items are straight up numbers or if they involve a variable.

2 **The relationship between degrees and radians is that 180 degrees equals pi radians.**

So, for example, if something was rotated pi radians, that is the same thing as saying that it was rotated 180 degrees.

3 **The word "respectively" allows you to know that the order that something was said is the order that you need to keep things in.**

So if it was stated that there were purple, blue, and pink flowers, and there were 30, 80, and 50 of them *respectively*, it means that there are 30 purple flowers, since the first color mentioned was purple and the first number that was mentioned was 30. It would also mean that there are 80 blue flowers, since both blue and 80 were mentioned second. And lastly, there are 50 pink flowers.

4 **A *horizontal asymptote* can be determined by using the lead coefficients of both the top and bottom of a given fraction.**

>   Ex. $3x^2 - 11x + 18 \;/\; 2x^2 + 4x - 9$

The horizontal asymptote in this case would be at 3/2, because the lead coefficient of the top of the fraction was 3, and the lead coefficient of the bottom of the fraction was 2. Whatever the lead coefficients are, you will simply put one over the other.

There are more complicated ways to determine horizontal asymptotes, but happily, the ACT does not seem interested in testing you on those more complicated ways.

5 **A standard system of equations is when you are given two equations and two variables. There are two classic ways to solve a standard system, one of which is referred to as "elimination".**

The "elimination" technique involves multiplying one or both of the given equations so that you can smoothly eliminate one of the two variables.

    Ex. $2x - y = 7$
                $5x + 2y = 4$

Given this system, you could multiply the top equation by 2. The idea behind doing so is that you are setting things up so that you can eliminate 'y'.

Multiplying the top equation by 2, you get a new top equation of $4x - 2y = 14$. Adding that equation to the other existing equation, the '-2y' and the '2y' cancel each other out, leaving you only with $9x = 18$, which allows you to determine that 'x' is 2. From here, if you needed to get the value of 'y', you could do so by plugging in 'x' as 2 into either of the original equations.

6 **A repeating decimal is indicated by a line going across the top of the numbers that are repeating.**

So if you had a decimal like ".26" with a line above both the 2 and the 6, then the decimal really is a decimal that would be a never-ending run of 2's and 6's, as partially illustrated by this: .2626262626

Keep in mind that only the numbers with a line above them repeat. So if you had a decimal like ".257" with a line only above the 5 and the 7, then the decimal is one that starts with a 2 and then has a never-ending run of 5's and 7's, as partially illustrated by this: .25757575757

7 **Within circles, a given sector of a circle or a given arc length of part of a circle is directly related to the angle that creates the given sector or arc.**

So, for example, if you were given a circle and there was a 120-degree angle, then you would know that the sector area of that part of the circle would be one-third of the whole circle's area, since 120 degrees is one-third of a circle's total of 360 degrees.

In another example, if you were given a circle and there was an 80-degree angle, then you could say that the outside arc length of that part of the circle was 80/360 of the total circle's circumference.

8 **Similar to the previous point, if you are creating a circle graph, you would use a fraction and the idea that an entire circle is 360 degrees to determine how to construct any given part of the circle graph.**

For instance, if the part of a given budget allocated for decorations was $60 out of a $240 total budget, then (60/240) times 360 would be the angle measurement of the portion of the circle graph that the decorations would represent. In this case, the angle for the decorations would be a 90-degree angle.

9 **Factoring a quadratic that has a lead coefficient that is NOT an imaginary 1 requires some trial and error.**

$$\text{Ex.} \quad 2x^2 + x - 6 \longrightarrow (2x \quad)(x \quad)$$

If you were trying to factor something like what is above, you could start by splitting off a '2x' and an 'x' into separate parentheses. From here, you would need to try different number options until you found the exact one that makes everything work.

If it's been a really long time since you've factored, you would need to remember that the two numbers that go inside of the parentheses must multiply to equal -6. The need for trial and error in this situation arises because there are various ways to multiply to get -6, and where you put each number changes what happens.

If you were to put a -6 with the '2x' and a +1 with the 'x' and then FOIL everything out, you would not get what was originally there. If you were to put a +3 with '2x' and a -2 with the 'x', you would also not get what was originally there.

Only the lone correct option of putting a -3 in with the '2x' and a +2 with the 'x' yields the proper result.

10 **Let's talk about a quirky aspect of fractions that the ACT has tested before.**

If you want to make a fraction as *small* as possible, then you want the denominator to be as *big* as possible.

Conversely, if you want to make a fraction as *big* as possible, then you want the denominator to be as *small* as possible.

This inverted way of thinking can make a potential question tricky at first, but once you have this idea in hand, you should be in great shape if the ACT throws this in another question in the future.

11 **A standard situation involving *compound interest* will likely be in terms of years.**

Given that this is true, if a different compound interest situation mentioned that the interest involved was getting "compounded monthly", then you should see a 12 within the given equation, since there are 12 months in a year.

If yet another compound interest situation mentioned that the interest involved was getting "compounded weekly", then you should see a 52 within the given equation, since there are 52 weeks in a year.

12 **Multiplying matrices requires a series of steps. Happily, if you ever encounter a question on an ACT that requires you to multiply matrices, there is a good chance that you only need to do one set of calculations in order to determine the correct answer.**

Let's imagine you are dealing with two 2 by 2 matrices, which is almost definitely the biggest types of matrices an ACT question would ever give you if it was asking you to multiply.

The first thing you will do is multiply whatever is in the upper lefthand corner of the first matrix by whatever is in the upper lefthand corner of the other matrix. Then you will multiply whatever is in the upper righthand corner of the first matrix by whatever is in the bottom lefthand corner of the second matrix. You will then take the results of these two calculations and add them together. This value is what should be in the upper lefthand corner of the correct answer.

In the very off chance that a multiplying matrices question appears on your exam, what is mentioned above is all that you should likely need to do, as only one answer option will have the proper first value in the upper lefthand corner of the matrix of the correct answer.

13 **The complex number "i" has special properties associated to it. One of those properties is related to exponents, and happily, there is a pattern that can be memorized.**

$$i^1 = i \quad i^2 = -1 \quad i^3 = -i \quad i^4 = 1$$

This pattern then repeats as you increase the exponents.

$$i^5 = i \quad i^6 = -1 \quad i^7 = i \quad i^8 = 1$$

14 **The only trigonometric identity that you might want to memorize is the one that states that the sine of something squared PLUS the cosine of something squared is equal to 1.**

Seeing this in a more mathematical manner may help trigger a memory in your mind.

$$\sin^2(x) + \cos^2(x) = 1$$

15 **To determine the *period* of a trigonometric function, you need to divide either pi or 2pi by a given value within the function, depending on which of the six trig functions you are dealing with.**

For *tan* and *cot*, you take whatever value is in front of the variable and divide that into pi.

    Ex.   The period of g(x) = cot(6x) is pi/6

For *sin*, *cos*, *csc*, and *sec*, you take whatever value is in front of the variable and divide by 2pi.

    Ex.   The period of r(x) = sec(3x) is (2pi)/3 or (2/3)pi

Five Reasons to Skip

Now that we have covered a considerable amount of raw material, let's turn things back around toward the strategy side of test taking. And let's revisit what is maybe the single most important Math idea that we will ever discuss, Math Mantra #1: *Skip Around*.

Effectively skipping around is a way to guarantee that things go the way you want them to go on test day. It may take getting used to, like so many things when it comes to the ACT. To help you get an even firmer grasp on how to follow through nicely with Mantra #1, let talk about five classic reasons to skip a given question.

❶ *Because it's a "cluster block"...*

Not sure when it happened, but at some point I started calling certain questions *cluster blocks*.

Cluster blocks (CB) are questions that are grouped together, something that will be made clear right at the start of a CB. There will be a box at the start of a CB that states within it that you will "Use the following information..." to answer the questions that are clustered together. It appears that on every ACT, there be at least two or three CBs.

So now that you know what a CB is and that some are definitely coming, let's discuss why you should skip them. The rationale is simple: typically at least one question in the block is strange or is something that will require you to interpret something about it. So instead of engaging with the block of questions, only to then encounter a strange item that could pose a threat, skip the whole CB and keep your momentum moving in the right direction.

Now though I am telling you to initially skip CBs, I also want to tell you now that you absolutely do want to come back to them as well. As mentioned, there is almost always a question that is a threat within the CB, which is why we are skipping the entire block. However, there is also usually at least one question that is very straightforward, and we definitely want to get that question on test day.

One final comment to make about CBs is that there is an exception to our idea here of skipping past them. The exception is if the CB comes before question #20. It seems to be a thing that if a CB preceded #20, then it is quite possible that the whole block will be manageable. But again, any block after question #20, I do strongly advise skipping.

❷ Because of the type...

Some students dread word problems. Some students are definitely better at algebra than they are at geometry. Some students would rather walk on fire than do trigonometry.

Knowing that there are certain types of questions that you don't love is part of a sound test day game plan. Later, before we wrap up our Math conversation, we'll talk even more about the idea of embracing known weaknesses and about how you can score what you are dreaming of scoring and still skip a given question because of the type of question it happens to be.

❸ Because of its setup...

Some questions are just so long that even looking at them sucks a little life out of us on test day. Skipping past such a question seems like an excellent test day decision.

Some questions have a funky looking diagram or something within the setup that looks strange. Skipping past such a question seems like an excellent test day decision.

Remember, skipping is not a defeat. It is a way to maintain momentum. It is a way to instill within ourselves the clear sense that we are in control from the moment the section starts to the moment it finishes.

❹ Because it's 3-D geometry...

On most exams, there is only one 3-D geometry question. Whenever I encounter a 3-D geometry question, I skip it. My rationale is very simple: pretty much every 3-D geometry question is unique. How I solve one is not how I solve a different one. Given the uniqueness of each 3-D geometry question, I automatically skip them and come back to them later.

I don't want to do anything new on test day, not at least until I have already done what I already am very comfortable with. I don't want to have to come up with a unique solution to a single question when there are other questions that are coming up later that I already know have set ways to be solved.

If it turns out that the 3-D geometry question that I skip past doesn't require me to do anything crazy hard in order to solve it, great! But on the day of the real exam, why take a risk that I don't need to take? In short, I don't.

5. *Because it's in any way unfamiliar or uncomfortable...*

To close out our discussion here, let's maybe acknowledge what the whole point of this particular conversation about skipping has been about overall.

We want to maintain control over the Math section of the test. Therefore, it is sound test taking to skip any question for just about any reason. And so, a good final category/reason to skip a question can be a catch-all idea like skipping any question that makes you in any way uncomfortable or that is unfamiliar.

If you've made it to this part of the book, then you've likely read through a lot of mathematical concepts. This means that on test day, there will be questions that you know that you can handle, questions that reward the preparation that you put into this process. Knocking those questions out and leaving less familiar questions for later is a game plan that breeds positive momentum and confidence.

The plan is to maintain control over the Math section of the test. Actually, the plan is to maintain control throughout the ACT. From the moment the proctor tells us to open the test booklet and begin working on Section 1 to the 10-minute break after the Math section to the last moments of Science when most of us are still working, we can be in control.

We got this my friend. Let's meditate on some final Math ideas.

Seven Math Meditations

A few more ideas to square away to make sure that your Math mentality is as fortified as possible. Then we'll talk about some targets and expectations and just like that more ACT fun will have blinked by!

1. The First 20

As we've already spoken about, it is impossible for the ACT to really have a clear order of difficulty within the Math section of the test. That said, it does seem like the first 20 questions or so are generally going to skew toward the more manageable side of the spectrum.

So if Math is NOT your favorite part of the ACT, then it's super important for you to tackle the first 20 questions super slowly and carefully. There will undoubtedly be questions that you can comfortably handle past #20, but if you lay a strong enough foundation through the first third of the section, then you're simply giving yourself that much more breathing room throughout the rest of the section.

And for those of you who don't mind the Math portion of the test, or maybe even like this part of the test, don't take the first 20 questions for granted. I am acknowledging that they skew toward the more manageable side. That doesn't mean that all of them will be simple and that you shouldn't still adhere to Math Mantra #1.

2. Embrace Your Weaknesses

I told you we were going to talk more about this idea, and we're doing so because it is potentially a major part of how you will crush the ACT comes test day.

A monster test taker can recognize something that she saw in practice that she did NOT like. Accordingly, she will skip this item if she saw it on test day and potentially come back to it. A powerful test taker knows that he can consciously avoid certain types of questions. He can pick and choose his battles and still turn every dream into a reality.

We'll soon be talking about particular score targets. Until then, fully embrace the idea that on test day, you can (and should) embrace some of your weaknesses.

3. Expect Oddballs

My definition of an "oddball" is any question that would be close to impossible to re-create. Oddballs are questions that you cannot immediately recognize as something that you have done before. And therefore, you would need to react to oddballs on the spot if you were hoping to correctly answer a given one.

With enough experience, recognizing an oddball can be quite manageable. If you spot one on test day, the best decision is likely to skip it and come back to it. As we have spoken about already, why take a risk on test day. We know oddballs are coming, so the only question is how you will choose to deal with them. Getting caught up on an oddball, which can lead to frustration, is something that you can choose to avoid.

4. One More Step

A classic standardized test thing to do is to potentially fool you into not realizing there is still *one more step*.

For instance, you solve a given equation for the given variable, let's say in this case, 'x'.

But, the final question isn't asking you for 'x'.

There may be one final thing that you need to do. For instance, maybe you need to take what you just got for 'x' and pop it back into an equation within the given question and determine the value of 'y', which is what the final question is actually asking for.

Or maybe, there will be something that you need to kind of "flip" within the question. Knowing that there may be a question or two that requires that *one more step* may be all you need to ensure that everything goes as smoothly as possible on test day.

5. A Capped Out "NOT"

Were you wondering what I meant by something that you might need to "flip" in the previous meditation?

A classic example would be a question tied to probability that ends up asking you what the probability is for something "NOT" to happen. Reading such a question a touch too quickly could obviously lead you to simply finding the probability of whatever the question was mentioning versus the probability of that something NOT happening.

A potentially simple way to make sure that a capped out "NOT" does not sneak by you would be to circle it if it happens to appear within a question.

6 The Wording Matters

Building off of the previous meditation, let's acknowledge the general importance of the wording of just about any question. And let's acknowledge that the more well prepared you are, the less the clock is going to matter to you. If you know what to do, you really will have the time to do it.

So, having made these acknowledgments, please don't ever rush the way you read a given Math question, because the wording of the question definitely matters. And on the day of the real exam, it is very easy to gloss over something or read something wrong.

A question could mention the "diameter", but you may need to remember to chop that value in half because what a given question might require you to actually use is the radius. A different question might ask you to determine the perimeter of a given shape, but your brain could be on autopilot and before you know it, you are calculating the shape's area. Hopefully, just even pointing out the simple idea of how important the wording of a question is will lead you to making fewer mistakes on the day of your real exam.

7 The Last 10

Like all standardized tests, the ACT does punish sloppy work and a lack of attention to detail. So if you figure out the perimeter of a given shape, when what the question wanted was the area, it's not surprising at all that what you got for the perimeter will still be one of the listed answer options.

I don't see listing the perimeter as an answer option, when what the question wanted was the area, as a trick or a trap. It is simply the nature of a classically written standardized test question.

However, it does seem like every so often, the ACT does throw in the rare "trap" question. But happily, if it does do so within a given exam, it only seems to happen once, and it would be somewhere within the final 10 questions.

So what this final meditation is trying to forewarn you that if you think an answer to a question that is past #50 seems a bit too straightforward and a bit too obvious, it may be because it is too straightforward and too obvious. If you can figure out what's really happening within the question, wonderful. And if you can't, maybe just guess something other than the answer that you think is too obvious to be the correct answer.

Targets & Expectations

Now that we've made it to the end of our Math discussion, let's acknowledge something that might be surprising: even if you love Math, your English score might end up higher than your Math score.

What?!

Or maybe, you're not surprised by that comment. Because you noticed that I mentioned more than once within the English portion of the book that the English section of the ACT is the most preparable aspect of basically all standardized tests that exist.

Now this is not to say that you cannot diligently prepare for the Math section of the ACT. I just need you to know the reward for your hard work is just not necessarily as immediate. What is tested within the English section is so remarkably consistent. Within the Math section, there is simply a much wider range of material that the ACT draws from, and there is much less consistency with what gets tested from one test to the next.

Accordingly, a superior test taker goes into the exam with a clear sense of what he might actually need to target to achieve his ultimate goal. An incredible test taker knows that she can afford for certain questions to be unfamiliar and uncomfortable, so she will simply fill in a random answer to such questions and calmly move on.

Ok, so let's get a sense of what your targets and expectations for Math may be.

▶ *24-26*

If you absolutely dread math in general, it would not be unusual at all to score below this range, especially if it was prior to reading LTSA!

However, I firmly believe that you can work to get into this range. If you detest this portion of the test, I'm not saying it will be easy to do so. But I know that with enough time, experience, and memorization of certain key ideas and facts, you can get here.

To give you a clear sense, to hit this initial score threshold, you basically need to feel confident that you can do HALF of the 60 questions. Anything that you don't know, you will put a random answer for, since there is no penalty for getting any questions wrong on the ACT.

In case you are surprised (which I would kind of understand if you were), what I just wrote is NOT a typo! To get to this level, which is certainly not a simple thing for many of us to do, it basically takes knowing that you can crush HALF of the 60 questions. So know the Mantras, and in particular, have a really firm grasp on Mantra #1 and embrace the art of *skipping around*. Flat out memorize everything that you "MUST" memorize. Understand the most of the Meditations, know as much as you can of what you should "TRY" to memorize, and basically ignore the ugly stuff that is within the "CHOOSE" to memorize category.

I know you don't love math. But you don't need to in order to beat the Math on the ACT. We got this.

▶ *27-29*

If you don't despise math, then I am confident you can get to this level, which is certainly way above the national average.

To get here, you need to feel confident that you can crush 40 of the 60 questions. Not sure if that is a surprising statement, but to be crystal clear: there could be 20 questions that you are uncomfortable with and you can score within this range. This should potentially be a very stress-relieving amount of leeway.

To ensure that you can confidently crush 40 questions, try to have everything memorized and understood within this part of the book other than what's in the "CHOOSE" section. Obviously, if you can pick up some of that material as well, that would be amazing. But a superior test taker does understand when it might be better to not overwhelm himself with too much information.

▶ *Breaking 30*

If you have a natural comfort level with math, then it makes sense that your personal goal is to break 30. Maybe the key to doing so is realizing that you also have what might be a surprising degree of leeway to not know certain questions on test day.

There could be up to 10 questions that you are uncomfortable with and the dream of breaking 30 wouldn't be a dream. Knowing that there could be this many questions that you don't need to be able to do, don't let your inner nerd screw things up. Don't get stuck on questions. Skip around like the rest of us and stay in control of the test.

Oh, and try to know and memorize as much within this part of the book as possible. But also keep in mind that you don't need to know it all. Obviously, right?

▶ *32-34*

I know that for a good number of my readers, breaking 30 just isn't enough. So if you are one of those who needs to be *in* the 30s and not merely right past it, then let's talk about what your latitude may be on test day.

At the highest end of the scoring spectrum, things are a bit more volatile, as the ACT does slightly adjust what number of correct leads to what precise score on different exams. That said, a good general target to keep in mind is that there can typically be about 5 questions that you don't love on test day and this score goal can still be smoothly achieved.

If you're reading this, you obviously kind of like math, or at the very least, you've gotten very good at ACT Math. Knowing that, I need to forewarn you to not be stubborn. On every live ACT I have ever personally taken, I have skipped *at least* 5 questions as I was working my way through the entire section. I go back and do those questions later, because I am always pushing to score a perfect 36.

Wonderfully, you don't need a perfect 36 in Math in order to make whatever college dream you are dreaming a reality. So don't even blink when it comes time to skip past a certain question or two or five.

▶ *35 or 36*

Hello my very nerdy friend who is reading this. I address you as a compatriot, for I too am a proud nerd. But let's not talk of nerdery right now. Let us talk about what maybe separates the two of us.

I will always score within this range. To be even more obnoxious, I basically have gotten a perfect 36 in Math every time I have taken a live ACT. (I lost track because there have been so many 36s, but maybe I got a 35 once.)

Why I want to be so obnoxious right now is to reinforce how important it is to acknowledge that even as a person taking the ACT who expects to score a perfect 36 each time out in Math, I still expect bumps in the road. I expect there to be a question that I do not recognize. I follow Math Mantra #1 obsessively. On certain exams, I have skipped more than 10 questions. I came back and did them all, but I still skipped them so that I didn't allow myself to feel as if I was not firmly in control of the section.

I make the ACT do what I want it to do. And I do that by respecting how challenging it is designed to be. So don't allow yourself to get stuck on a question. Realize that you can score a perfect 36 and actually miss a question. Don't be stubborn like so many nerds tend to be when it comes to a test like the ACT. And, oh yeah, memorize everything within this part of the book my nerdy friend.

Reading

Four Mantras

① *Choose Your Order*

There will be four passages, each with ten questions, to potentially do on test day. Very simply, it would be silly to do them in the order that they happen to be placed.

The first passage should always be a story, an excerpt from an actual novel. I would highly advise NOT doing the first passage first. The rationale is simple. A story could require you to interpret something. A character within the story might say something sarcastically. If you don't interpret something correctly or if you don't catch the potential sarcasm, you could be getting off to an uncertain start.

Get off to an amazing start by first choosing to do one of the three passages that come after the story! It should only take seconds to quickly flip through the section and get a sense of what's what. When your proctor tells you to open your booklet to section three and begin, the first thing you'll do is flip right past the first passage, since we already know it's a story. You'll peek at the other three readings, find one that you think may be the most interesting to you, and now you can rock and roll.

Something to note before we move on is that I am not telling you to do the story passage last. I am simply telling you not to do it first. If you think you'll like the story, doing it second can be a great game plan for you. If you think you will hate the story, then doing it last most certainly makes sense. Personally, I always do the story passage third.

② *Bail As Needed*

Let's now imagine that you have chosen your first reading, the one that you thought was going to be the most interesting. Maybe you selected the passage that you are doing first by taking a quick peek at the first line or two and seeing that the given passage was going to be about an animal.

But after reading through the first ten lines or so, you start to realize that the passage isn't turning out to be as interesting as you thought. Or maybe, the passage isn't turning out to really be about what you thought it was going to be about.

So bail out my friend and choose to do a different passage instead.

As long as you haven't read past line 15 or so, you have not invested that much time, and so bailing out and moving to a different reading is a sound decision. If you have made it past line 15 or so, and things seem to be going fine, then odds are there will be no issue as you continue to read.

The whole point of the first mantra is that we want to get off to a great start. Our second mantra is here to ensure that you really, really do get off to a great start. It is certainly not impossible that a particular passage doesn't turn out to be what you thought it would be, and I wanted to be sure that you knew that if that happened on test day, you're certainly not stuck.

Lastly, this idea of bailing as needed would certainly apply at basically any point within the Reading section. So if you have completed one passage and have started your second passage, and then ten lines into that one you want to change your mind and bail, then do not hesitate to do so my friend.

③ *Write Notes*

So you chose your order, and you haven't bailed. Now, let's acknowledge that the ACT isn't trying to do anything sketchy within the Reading part of the test. The ACT expects that your natural instinct will be to simply start by fully reading a given passage and then answering the questions that follow. Knowing what the ACT expects, I would advocate a very straightforward approach: just read the passage first as intended.

I imagine that previous statement was nothing surprising to read, though, you might be surprised that not everyone actually does just read the passage first. In any case, you are going to simply read the full passage first. And what I would strongly, STRONGLY advise you also do while you are reading is write notes. What does this mean?

On the day of a real exam, after reading a typical paragraph, I stop to write something down about what I have read. Sometimes I only write a word or two. Sometimes I write something that I think sums up the paragraph. Sometimes I write down what I think a paragraph did, versus what I think it was saying. Sometimes I just write down an exact word from the paragraph. Sometimes, if a paragraph is super long, I stop to write something down halfway through the paragraph. Sometimes, I write down the tone of a paragraph, simply noting that it was positive or negative.

There are so many benefits to writing notes. Writing notes will break up the boredom and monotony of reading through a painfully dull passage. Writing notes tends to force you to pay more attention. Some of the notes that you write will very possibly lead to direct answers to certain questions that you are later asked. There is no right or wrong in regards to what you write, but the physical act of writing notes definitely compels action that directly leads to sharper work on test day.

4. Trust Yourself

So, you chose the reading you wanted to start with. There was no need to bail, and you are writing notes while you are reading. And now you are done reading.

So now I want you to *trust yourself* to the appropriate degree.

Know that quite a few of the questions that were written by the ACT were most definitely designed to be ones that you could answer off the top of your head, assuming you had read the passage solidly well in the first place.

And given that you will read well on test day (helped by the fact that you are writing notes), don't be surprised if you feel confident that you can answer many of the ten questions that accompany a given reading without going back to the original passage. How many is many? I have definitely encountered passages in which students have felt confident that they knew the answers to nine of the ten questions without making any additional reference back to the passage.

More generally, it appears that for nearly every ACT Reading passage, a good read will lead to you knowing at least half of the answers to the questions off the top of your head. We need to talk more about this, and we will be immediately. For now, we simply needed to establish this fourth and final mantra.

Find Your Balance

I would typically not talk about score targets and expectations until the end of a given section of a book. But specifically for the ACT Reading section, it really makes sense to have part of the discussion now.

Something that you likely don't already know is that you can achieve a Reading score of 28 without finishing one entire passage. For many people, I would think this is pretty shocking information.

What we need to do now is use that information appropriately, because different students are obviously in very different situations. There is a balance that you need to find, and that balance should be different depending on your situation.

And so now, my friend, maybe read only one of the three things that are about to follow.

▶ *Your Reading Score is Under 28*

If you have already taken the ACT and your Reading score is under 28, I want you to know that you can improve your score and not have the Reading section of the test feel like a race to finish.

The timing of the Reading section was definitely designed to be a challenge. I believe the ACT consciously understands that it writes questions that are not crazy complex and technically impossible. But the ACT also understands that if it puts a standard time limit of 35 minutes on the section, that time limit will cause some serious problems for many, many students.

So here again is some amazing news. If you are currently under 28, you can get to 28 without even getting to one entire block of questions. Your emphasis right now should be on quality. You should be learning how to make sure you get questions correct, and if your timing comes around naturally, then great. But if it doesn't, you may be able to see a huge jump in your score without ever needing your timing to come around.

The balance that you need to strike right now needs to lean heavily toward the side of being laser focused on simply getting questions done correctly and basically giving zero thought to the clock. Read carefully, write notes, go back to the passage to confirm that you have the correct answer just about anytime you feel like you need to, and get nearly every question correct in whatever Reading passage you happen to be working on.

▶ Your Reading Score is 28 or Higher

If you already have a score that is 28 or higher, in order for your score to likely reach its maximum potential, you will likely need to fully embrace Mantra #4.

You couldn't score as high as you have already scored if you didn't have a solid natural feel for quite a bit of what you're being tested on within the Reading portion of the exam. And so, I need you to trust yourself to the proper degree to ensure that you can tackle each of the 40 questions without feeling rushed.

There is a delicate balance to be struck here.

There are some questions that clearly require any normal human to go back to the passage and simply be sure that he has found the correct answer. But then there are other questions that you need to trust that you really do know the answers to, choose what you think is correct without going back to the passage, and assertively move on. And there may even need to be the occasional question that you need to recognize is oddly throwing you off. And with such a question, the proper decision is likely to not dwell on the question. We'll talk more about this later.

The balance that you need to strike is one that still places a properly heavy emphasis on accuracy, but one that also acknowledges the need to be appropriately decisive when dealing with any given question. There's more for us to talk about, but keep this idea of balance in mind my friend.

▶ You Reading Score Doesn't Exist

If you are heading into your first ACT, which is why you have a non-existent Reading score, there is a balance that you are also trying to find, but it isn't one that you need to be overly conscious of yet.

As you read more of this part of the book, I suspect some things in regards to the balance that you will eventually strike will naturally materialize. But again, for now, I would advise that you don't give those things, whatever they may be, much conscious thought.

Flat out memorize what's about to follow. Do your best to embrace the techniques that will come after that. Go into your first exam with a good amount of knowledge about the Reading portion of the ACT. And then, once you get your first score, we can make some additional adjustments my friend.

Things You MUST Memorize

The Reading portion of the ACT isn't really about memorization. It is more about execution and finding the proper balance between pushing to finish enough of the questions while still maintaining an appropriate level of accuracy.

That said, there are some things that you really must just memorize. And given how few things are about to follow, I think you maybe know the deal by now. If you are not going to flat out memorize what's about to come, then why are you even reading this book?!

1. The Five Problem Words

If you see any of these five words within an answer option to a Reading question, the likelihood that that option is the correct answer is incredibly super low.

So what I am basically telling you is that you should feel very, very confident crossing out any answer that contains any of these five words.

most   only   best   first   worst

That's it. It's only these five words. Simple enough, right?

2. A Vocab Word

Very wonderfully, vocabulary is simply not really a part of the ACT. As you'll read later in the Mediations for this chapter, generally, if you run across something that you don't know, like a particular word, for instance, it's wise to simply keep reading and not worry about it.

That said, here is a word that you should just memorize.

refute - to argue against

There are other legitimate definitions of this word, but the definition above is the one that I would recommend memorizing.

③ The Three Trust Words

Do you already have Mantra #4 memorized?

No worries if you don't, as it is only a matter of time before you do.

Mantra #4: *Trust Yourself* is an important aspect of how you will strike the ideal balance within this part of the exam on test day. So let's talk about now the following three words.

infer *mainly* *primarily*

If you see any of these three words within a Reading question, there is a very solid chance that you may already know the answer to the question, so you should likely trust yourself and go straight to the answer options and see if you really do know the answer.

Things You Should TRY to Memorize

Given how manageable it likely will be for you to memorize what came before this, it would be pretty awesomely fantastic if you picked up a good amount of what's about to come within this part of the book.

That said, if some of this doesn't stick, well, that's why this is the "TRY" part of the unit versus the "MUST".

1. Short Answers

Let's build on where we left off in the previous part. Another instance in which you might want to *trust yourself* and see if you happen to know the answer to a given question is when the answer options are short.

The logic behind this is simple: when the answers are short, you can evaluate them rather quickly. So if you go straight to the answer options when they are short, if you do end up knowing the answer off the top of your head, you will likely realize that you do rather quickly.

And, of course, if after reading a given set of short answer options, if you are not sure what to choose, then go back to the passage and take your time to find the correct answer.

2. Line References

Continuing a theme we are building, let's now acknowledge that when a given question mention specific line references, this is NOT an automatic indication that you need to go back to those lines.

Now, for so many of students, there is, of course, nothing wrong with going back to any mentioned lines. As we have already spoken about, there is a balance that each of us needs to individually strike between accuracy and timing. So if it makes you more confident and comfortable to basically always go back to given lines when they are referenced, then that is what you should do.

However, if you do feel like you might know the answer to a given question that references some specific lines, you should not be shocked. I have definitely seen many questions that had particular line references that did seem designed to be answered without actually going back to the given lines.

3. Wrong Part, Wrong Answer

Let's introduce a skill that we will most certainly revisit later within this part of the book. The idea of *wrong part, wrong answer* is a perfect way to ease into this concept.

The savviest test takers are the ones that can identify classic wrong answers, because happily, the ACT really does craft very consistent types of wrong answers. Maybe the simplest to start to get accustomed to noticing is the wrong answer that mentions something that is clearly stated within the passage, but it is from a different part of the passage than what we need for a given question.

To be crystal clear, let's imagine that a question asks you about something that you know was referenced toward the end of a given passage. A classic wrong answer would be one that you know was definitely mentioned in the passage, but maybe, it was toward the middle of the passage.

This is a classic type of wrong answer that the ACT crafts, knowing that students will be tempted to choose it, since it is clearly something that was mentioned within the passage. That said, because of our beloved Mantra #3: *Write Notes*, I think it should be quite manageable for you to dodge this classic wrong answer. Having written notes, you will likely have a strong handle on what was said at various stages within any given passage.

Things You CHOOSE to Memorize

Now we enter the realm of material that maybe you don't even need to be reading my friend. For your dream to not be just a dream, it may be important for you to pick and *choose* your battles, and what's about to follow may not be what you need to choose to acquire.

Isn't it nice to feel in charge of your preparation?

1. Distortions

With this first item in the "Choose" section of this part of the book, we're building off of where we left off in the "Try" section. Let's talk about another classic type of wrong answer, one that is potentially a touch trickier to notice.

A *distortion* is an answer option that is relevant, because it does bring up material that is clearly mentioned within a given Reading passage. The problem is that something about that material is slightly off or possibly significantly different than what was actually mentioned within the passage.

For instance, a passage could mention how a specific experiment "could be conducted in the future." A wrong answer option that we would consider a *distortion* would potentially make an alteration to that statement by indicating that a certain experiment has already yielded some insights. Such an alteration would make it seem like that experiment has already been conducted, which is not what was originally stated within the passage.

Distortions are tempting answer options precisely because they do reference something that clearly was mentioned within the passage. And given how subtle some of them can be, it definitely is understandable if you don't always seem them hiding within a given set of answer options. So keep these items in mind as you are continuing to build your ACT skill set, but don't go too crazy about them. This is why they are kicking off the "Choose" part of this section of the book!

2. "More recently, however,"

Very occasionally, a phrase might appear within a given passage that has such a distinct meaning, it would be awesome if you happened to notice it.

Referencing the title of this particular point, a phrase such as "More recently, however," clearly has a very particular meaning. Such a phrase indicates a very clear transition within a given passage. The passage is definitely going to transition from discussing whatever was being mentioned prior to the use of that phrase to something that is about to contrast what had just been mentioned.

If you happen to notice a phrase like this within a given passage, it would make sense to circle it within the passage. Significant transitions like this tend to be referenced at some point within a question or two.

3. A Minor Trap

I like to mention that the Reading section within the ACT is really not trying to ever trick testers. This is a very straightforward aspect of the exam, though, the timing of the section can be a challenge.

For the most part, the ACT is presenting you with material that you might find boring, but it is not trying to do anything crazy clever to mislead you. If you read well, which you will since you'll be writing notes, you will be well positioned to tackle the vast majority of the questions that you are presented with.

That said, every so often, the ACT does get a little crafty, so don't be shocked if you see something that seems a touch clever. For instance, if you were asked what the purpose of the last sentence of a paragraph was, it would be natural for people to assume that it might be to "summarize". However, a final sentence to a given paragraph can certainly be used to do a multitude of things, such as transition the passage from one paragraph to the next.

Happily, you really don't need to be very concerned about the presence of a minor trap within a given Reading section, as many Reading sections will not have anything that even remotely would be considered a trap.

Four Specialty Questions

1. The "most nearly means" Question (MNM)

Potential Frequency:

It would seem as if you can expect to see this type of question pretty much once on every exam.

Priority Level:

Even though there will likely only be one MNM on the entire test, it is such a straightforward thing to discuss that you should just memorize what is mentioned next.

Fundamental Idea/Approach:

We're starting with this item because it is a perfect way to ease into this part of the book that deals with specific specialty questions found within the Reading section of the test.

You will easily recognize this type of question because the exact words of "most nearly means" should be within the question.

The approach to this question type is simple: replace whatever word(s) that is *italicized* within the question with each of the given answer options. Ideally, the correct answer will just sound correct to you and smoothly replace what was italicized within the question.

To give yourself the best shot at simply hearing the correct answer, it would make sense to read at least the full sentence that contains the italicized item from the question.

The Next Level:

If among the given four options, there is a word that you do not know, the best thing to do would be to leave the answer option that contained the unknown alone. Do NOT simply cross it off because you do not know what that given answer option means.

You should execute the primary approach and read through the other choices that contain words that you do recognize. Hopefully, one of those options will be the correct answer, and you can select what you think sounds best and forever ignore the word that you did not know.

On the other hand, if none of the choices that you recognize really feel right to you, the correct course of action could be to choose the option that contained the word that you do not know.

This is not a comfortable thing for many students to do. Happily, there is a very good chance that this circumstance does not even arise on test day. So if this comment doesn't deeply resonate with you, no worries my friend.

2. *The Main Purpose/Idea Question (MP)*

Potential Frequency:

It would seem like you should expect to encounter this type of question at least once every exam. And it would certainly not be strange if it popped up twice.

Priority Level:

You should also flat out memorize what is about to be said here, as none of it is anything heavy duty.

Fundamental Idea/Approach:

A typical MP will likely literally have the words "main purpose" or "main idea" within the question.

Knowing that you are following through with other core Reading ideas, particularly the strategy of writing notes, then it should not surprise you at all to read that you should expect yourself to already know the answer to an MP off the top of your head. To somewhat reiterate what was just said: there should be no need to refer back to the passage in order for you to answer an MP.

The Next Level:

Throughout the Reading portion of LTSA, we refer to types of wrong answers. A superior test taker goes into her exam knowing the various types of wrong answers the ACT test writers tend to craft.

A classic type of wrong answer to be found within the given options for an MP is an answer that is *too specific*.

So, if you tackling an MP and you are thinking that a given answer choice is clearly relevant, since it was discussed within the passage, but it is too specific to only one aspect of the given passage, don't be surprised. By test day, it would be wonderful if you felt very confident identifying such a classic wrong answer and felt great about decisively eliminating it.

③ The Paragraph Question (PQ)

Potential Frequency:

It would seem like you should expect to see this type of question at least two times, and it is certainly possible for it to appear even more frequently.

Priority Level:

Given what we were just talking about within the MP, it should be a zero issue for you to also pick up what's about to be said here. So definitely do so my friend!

Fundamental Idea/Approach:

The PQ should be very manageable to identify. The question will very likely flat out ask you what the "main idea" of a particular paragraph is. And the paragraph should also be directly identified by exact lines mentioned within a set of parentheses.

Given that a PQ is asking about an entire paragraph, it is quite possible that you do already know the answer and that there is no need to go back to the passage. This is certainly made more likely by the fact that you are obviously going to be following our beloved Reading Mantra #3: *Write Notes* on the day of your real exam.

And along those lines, since you are writing notes basically for every paragraph, you could certainly take a peek back at whatever note you had written for the paragraph being referenced.

The Next Level:

Just like with MPs, PQs will also have a classic wrong answer that falls within the category of being *too specific*. So as you are reading through the various answer options, if there is a choice that you do remember was clearly mentioned within a given paragraph, but it seems too specific to be the main idea of the entire paragraph, you should feel confident knocking that option out.

④ The Agree Question (AQ)

Potential Frequency:

It would seem like you should expect to see this question at least once, and possibly twice, within a given test. And it would specifically only appear within the Passage A/Passage B setup.

Priority Level:

Given what's about to follow is also pretty simple, it would certainly be awesome if you could just pick this one up too. That said, if it's starting to feel like a lot to memorize, then that's a legitimate concern when it comes to trying to effectively learn to speak ACT. So I encourage you to acquire what's about to follow, but it's not make or break.

Fundamental Idea/Approach:

So if you didn't already know, one of the four Reading passages will be set up with a Passage A and a Passage B. We are going to soon talk a bit more about the P-A/P-B passage.

Turning our attention specifically to the AQ, by nature, it can only appear within the P-A/P-B passage, since having two passages allows the ACT to ask what might be agreed upon. An AQ might flat out use the word "agree" within the question, which would make it clear you were dealing with an AQ. But without using the word "agree", a question would still be considered an AQ if it was asking you something that *both* passages did or thought.

The approach to an AQ is simple. Given that you will have read both passages and that you will have written notes, you should know the answer to an AQ without needing to go back to either passage. This is definitely a type of question in which you would want to trust yourself and go straight to the answer options.

The Next Level:

As I suspect you are becoming quite accustomed to doing now, let's transition this conversation toward a classic wrong answer, one that is particular to the AQ.

A classic wrong answer option that you can typically expect to find within an AQ is one that is one-sided. A one-sided answer is an option that very clearly seems to match one of the two passages, but whatever it is mentioning, isn't really found at all within the other passage. Such an option can be initially tempting since it so clearly connects to one of the two passages. But such an answer cannot be the right final option to choose if it is not something that both passages are capable of agreeing with.

Final Comment:

As we are about to close out our discussion of the Reading specialty questions, this feels like the perfect time to state something that is a bit of a wrap-up summary kind of thing.

And this is also a perfect bridge to the first of our Reading Meditations.

At the end of the P-A/P-B passage, there will likely be three total questions that ask you about both Passage A and Passage B. Like the specific AQ that we have been talking about here, there is a very good chance that you could answer all of these questions without going back to either passage.

So if you are looking to push your Reading balance a bit more toward the aggressive side to try to give yourself the opportunity to finish more of the questions, the questions that ask you about both passages would be an opportunity to do so.

Nine Reading Meditations

These Meditations are perfect things to read the night before the exam. They're also perfect to read once you've made it through some other key aspects of the book, like the Mantras.

We are beating the ACT by learning some key facts. And we are also beating the ACT by getting our minds right. And the bottom line is that we are beating the ACT! On that note, let's head into this chapter's Meditations.

1) Passage A/Passage B

Something that should make clear logistical sense is that if and when you deal with the P-A/P-B passage, you should obviously begin by reading Passage A. Of course, while you are reading, you will be writing notes.

What might not have been your first thought, though, is that after you finish reading Passage A, you should then proceed right to the first few questions, as there are questions that are solely about Passage A. Knock out those questions while the only thing in your head is Passage A.

After completing all of the questions tied solely to Passage A, you should then go ahead and read Passage B. After you have read Passage B and written more notes, you can then tackle all remaining questions.

2) Tone

After you finish reading a given passage, a great thing to quickly ask yourself is what the overall tone of the reading was. Keep in mind that the tone could be positive, negative or neutral.

A very cool thing that is super reliable is that if the overall tone of a passage is positive, it would be very, very unlikely for a negatively toned answer to end up being the correct answer to any given question within the passage. Similarly, if the overall tone of a passage is negative, it would be very, very unlikely for a correct answer to be positively toned.

And continuing with this line of thinking, if a reading had a neutral tone, it would be very unlikely for a correct answer to have either a positive or negative tone.

③ Don't Rush

When taking tests like the ACT, there is a very natural urge to go faster. And particularly within the Reading section of the test, that urge can be hard to resist. But if you rush the way that you read, you'll likely only understand the passage less effectively than if you simply read at your normal pace.

And you definitely don't want to rush reading through any of the questions. If you read through a question too quickly and slightly misunderstand what it may be asking, then things with that question are already derailed.

You're not trying to make anything go artificially faster that kind of can't be made to go artificially faster. A true test taking master is not fast; she or he is efficient and decisive.

④ Be Efficient and Decisive

Building off the previous Meditation, and tying together ideas that we have been talking about throughout this portion of the book, there are times within this part of the test when you should be appropriately decisive and appropriately aggressive in order to be maximally efficient.

Because you are reading well, versus reading fast, you are well equipped to attack certain questions. And it is likely that as you gain more experience, there will be more questions that you feel confident that you can answer without going back to the actual passage. To the right degree, you need to embrace this confidence, and doing so could translate into several behaviors.

For a certain question, you might feel tempted to go back to the passage, but instead, you choose to go right to the choices and trust that you do indeed already know the answer. For a different question, you might read answer option (B) and really feel that it is the correct answer. For the sake of maximal efficiency, a potentially acceptable corner to cut would be to choose this answer and not even read the remaining two choices.

As we have spoken about already, there is an appropriate balance to be struck. Part of the ideal balance is weighted toward being justifiably aggressive and decisive.

⑤ Know Yourself

As the last two Meditations should have made clear, there is a delicate balance to be struck. So to be sure that you are finding your own personal balance within the Reading portion of the test, you do want to monitor certain things and really get to know yourself in terms of this section of the exam.

For instance, there are clearly some Reading questions that require you to flat out find the correct answer within the passage. The correct answers to such questions turn out to be basically word for word restatements of a particular part of the passage. Missing such a question is an indication that your balance is off and that you are moving too quickly.

Something else that you want to learn about yourself is whether fact-based passages, which could be three of the four passages, are better for you regardless of what they happen to be about. A reading about the government might be excruciatingly boring, but because it doesn't require you to interpret anything, it might also be a passage you can end up crushing and getting nearly every question correct.

As you'll read about toward the very end of this book, when you are doing any practice work, it shouldn't really be about timing yourself or trying to simulate test day conditions that kind of can't be simulated anyway. What your practice work should be about, particularly when it comes to Reading, is discovering what works best for you and refining how you are approaching different aspects of the ACT.

6 *Practicing the "Why"*

At multiple junctures within this part of the book, we have spoken about classic types of wrong answers. Now, let's mention another one to keep in mind, and then, more importantly, let's pull some ideas together into a cohesive mindset and practice plan.

Taking a distortion, which is mentioned within the "Choose" section, one step further, you do occasionally see an answer choice that is the complete opposite of the correct answer. It might seem strange that the ACT would include such answers, but it actually makes quite a bit of sense. If you too quickly read an answer that is the complete opposite of what you want, you could easily misread it, and therefore, actually select it.

If you are hoping to really refine your work and hone your Reading abilities, a wonderful thing to do is to push yourself to articulate what precisely is wrong with a given choice. This is where the title of this Meditation comes from. Sometimes, you should likely be able to give a name to what you are seeing within a given wrong answer. Other times, you might pinpoint a word or two within a given wrong answer that makes you feel that a choice is incorrect. Either way, it is a clear sign that you are building ACT-crushing skills when you can better articulate what's compelling you to cross a given answer out.

7 *Ignore What You Don't Know*

Almost all of us are going to run across a word or a given sentence from a particular passage that we don't know or don't understand.

The best thing to do when this happens is to ignore what you don't know or don't understand and keep moving. The idea here is simple: no single word or line will likely affect your overall understanding of a given passage.

Maybe even more important to acknowledge is what would be your alternative anyway? Reading something a second time that you didn't understand the first time is likely just a colossal waste of time.

8 Know If You're Beat

Building off of the previous Mediation, and before we head into our final one, let's discuss the idea that it's actually quite ok if you realize that you are dealing with a particularly tough question.

It will probably not happen very often, but occasionally, there is a Reading question that is clearly rather complex. As you gain more and more experience, I suspect that you will naturally notice if a given question is something that you are really uncomfortable with. It may be a bit surprising, but the proper thing to do if you encounter such a question is likely to simply recognize that you are dealing with an unusually tough question, choose an answer, and move on.

9 One Time Check

And so we have arrived at our final Reading Meditation and the only other time we will explicitly talk about checking the clock. As you likely have noticed, we haven't talked much about time management. In fact, it hasn't been a part of our primary dialogue since the end of the English portion of this book. But just like within the English portion of the test, during the Reading section, it is wise to do a one time check of the clock.

So, let's imagine that you chose which passage you wanted to do first. You read it, wrote notes, answered all of the questions and have bubbled in all of the answers for that passage. Now would be when you might do your one and only time check.

The standard time limit for the Reading section is 35 minutes. Now dividing that by four, since there are four passages, yields 8 minutes and 45 seconds, which for the sake of simplicity, we can round up to 9 minutes. This is our point of reference for the following categories.

▶ *Under 7*

So most of us will definitely NOT find ourselves within this zone. But if after completing your first passage, you find yourself within this time frame, then you can know that you are surprisingly ahead of the clock, and by a decent margin. This should mean then that you can feel comfortable going back to the passage for just about any question that you would like.

▶ *7 to 9*

This is the zone that I always find myself within. It translates to being able to complete all four passages, but it also means that I don't have a lot of wiggle room to do so. I will need to continue to strike the proper balance between going back to the passage for certain questions and trusting myself with other questions.

▶ *9 to 12*

This time frame means that you will probably not finish all of the questions. If you were hoping to answer all of the questions, then you would potentially need to make the adjustment of answering more questions off the top of your head. Or maybe you should accept the fact that you are not going to finish, because you don't need to finish in order for your score to end up where you want it to be. (We'll be talking even more about this shortly.

▶ *12 or more*

So finding yourself within this zone on test day means that you are definitely not going to finish all the questions, and that your target may be to complete three of the four passages. Depending on what your ultimate Composite goal might be, there is zero issue with being here. Knowing that you are not going to finish all of the questions, it becomes very important to be super accurate, so go back to the passage to find the correct answer basically as much as you need to.

Targets & Expectations

Ok, before we get into the details of what it typically takes to get to certain scores, let's form a bit of a bridge from where we just left off with the final Meditation.

For a few reasons, Reading is a bit of an oddball section compared to the other three major parts of the ACT. Therefore, before we establish some clear targets, let's discuss something that may be rather important for you.

The 5-Minute Protocol

Your proctor is supposed to announce when you are down to the final five minutes of the section. Knowing this, I need you to be ready to make an adjustment depending on where you are when that warning is given.

The idea is actually pretty simple. When the proctor announces that you are down to the last five minutes, if you are reading a given passage and are through less than half of the passage, then you should stop reading. The time it would take you to finish reading the passage would eat up most of the remaining time, leaving you with little to no time to actually then tackle any of the questions.

So what you should do is abandon the passage you are reading and see which question you might be able to attack without having read the entire passage. If you know the types of questions that typically pop up, then it should make sense that you without having read a given passage in its entirety, you could still deal with an MNM, for instance.

It should equally make sense that you would NOT want to tackle a Main Purpose(MP) question, but you could potentially tackle a Paragraph Question(PQ). You might also be able to tackle a question that references very specific lines. Hopefully, within those final five minutes, you could legitimately have a shot at about 3-5 questions, and then you would simply fill in any remaining bubbles for the questions that you are not able to directly approach. Generally, when you bubble in answers to questions that you don't actually have a chance to read through, it makes sense to simply choose any column and bubble straight down.

Ok, before we close out this portion of the book and discuss some targets and expectations, let me stress that there is a very good chance that you will not need to engage in this outlined 5-Minute Protocol. And to be crystal clear, if the proctor gives you the five minute warning, and you are just about done reading a given passage, then finish reading it. By doing so, you likely have a great chance to answer at least four or five questions aggressively (and accurately), since you were able to finish reading the passage as you typically do. On that note, let's talk numbers.

▶ 33 or higher

If you are trying to score into this highest of levels, it's simple: you should know everything within this portion of the book. Because everything within this portion of the book is what I know and what I do. It really is that simple, because after all, all I really am is a super prepared test taker.

And if you are trying to score within this range, then let me also tell you that you can typically afford to miss 2 or 3 question in total. That isn't a lot of room for error, but it is some room. Keep that in mind and definitely keep Meditation #8: *Know If You're Beat* in mind. The road to a crushingly good score sometimes requires a conscious sacrifice.

▶ 29 to 32

So let's start off by acknowledging that to score within this range, you don't have to finish every question. You'd have to get close, but you could technically have it be that you ended up needing to fill in some random answers to a small handful of questions. So if when the proctor calls five minutes, you still have a good number of questions left to do, don't panic. Be accurate with what you can assertively answer and rest easy knowing that you didn't need to finish.

If you are finishing comfortably within the standard time limit, then let me clue you in to the leeway you have from an accuracy standpoint. To score within this range, you can typically afford to miss 1 or 2 questions per passage. For instance, on a real exam, you could miss 6 total questions and score a 30.

▶ 26 to 28

It may still be shocking to read this, but if you remember back at the start of this portion of the book, we did indeed mention that you could score as high as somewhere within this range and only end up doing three of the four passages. You would need to be super accurate within each passage, which typically means missing no more than 1 question per passage. But if you could be that accurate, then for the passage that you don't actually get to, you could fill in one blocked out column.

Some students feel like they are giving up a bit by only doing three of the four passages. If you are one of them, then think about it this way. If you were hoping to get a Composite score of 30, you could easily afford to get a 27 in Reading if you got a 33 in English. A great test taker sees the big picture and can employ an overarching strategy that encompasses the entire scheme of the exam.

▶ 22 to 25

This is the final category to discuss, because there is no question that you can reach this range even if you despise the Reading portion of the test.

If this is the range that you ultimately end up targeting, then life is pretty simple for you when it comes to this part of the test. Your mission is all about accuracy. You don't need to ever come close to finishing all four passages. In fact, you could end up finishing two and a half passages, and as long as you were accurate, you would score within this range.

Follow core techniques, memorize some of what absolutely can be memorized, go back to the passage whenever you want, and scoring within this range should be locked up my friend.

Science

Four Mantras

1. Not Trying to Trick You

The ACT knows that the Science section is inherently intimidating for most students simply because so many of us do not feel naturally comfortable with science as a general subject matter. Add to that the fact that the Science section is always the fourth section, which means that for nearly all students, the fatigue is very real by the time we get to this portion of the test.

Happily, given these ideas, the ACT does NOT seem interested in trying to make your life more difficult by trying to trick you with cleverly crafted questions. If something seems instinctively right within a given question, there is an exceptionally super high chance that it is right. If something seems very straightforward and clear, it is because it is straightforward and clear.

2. Don't Read Until Necessary

The 35-minute standard time limit does not leave most of us any room to do things that are not absolutely necessary. Accordingly, don't read any of the written blurbs within any Science passage until it is absolutely necessary to do so. On test day, you will likely be very pleasantly surprised as to just how many questions there are that you can smoothly answer correctly without ever having read any of the written information that accompanies any given passage.

3. Be Max Out Efficient

Building off of the previous mantra, it's just going to be generally true for nearly all of us that we don't have a second to waste. So a theme within this mantra that we are going to develop together is making sure that we get through questions by expending the least amount of brain power.

We are trying to take the path of least resistance with every question. We are not trying to prove that we are generally smart in regards to the realm of science. We are going to prove that we are incredibly skilled and aware in regards to the ACT realm of Science.

4. Mark It Up

Questions within this portion of the test are incredibly nitpicky and a refined attention to detail is a must. To ensure that you make as close to zero mistakes as possible with questions that you are clearly capable of handling, it is a must to mark things up.

Draw lines, label bar and line graphs, circle key words on given axes, box out key terms that distinguish one graph from another, etc. The more you mark things up, the safer you will be on test day.

The Core Roadmap

Allow me to make a bold proclamation: if you follow through with everything that I outline within the Science portion of this book, you will score at least a 27 in Science.

Yeah, I said it. And now let me further elaborate: I believe that every dedicated student who follows the roadmap that is about to follow and everything else detailed within these Science pages can *earn* a score of at least 27.

Now, if you're reading this and you already have a 27 or higher, be assured, I have you covered as well. If you have a 27, we're going to get you to at least a 30. If you have a 30 already, let's get you into the 30s. If you're into the 30s already, then let's get you further into the 30s. If you have a 35 already, then I think reading what's here, you will have a real shot at a perfect 36. And if you have a perfect 36 already, what the hell are you doing reading this part of the book?!

I think we're ready to start to outline your core roadmap to Science success.

▶ Wave 1 (W1)

There are many Science questions that require you to have absolutely ZERO science knowledge. Physics could be a total enigma to you, as it is to me. You could have had a brutal biology teacher, as I did. You could have had a brilliant chemistry teacher (like I did!), but chemistry could still feel like ancient history because you took it last year.

Happily, these things can be true, but you can still destroy what we will call Wave 1 (W1) questions!

W1 questions are questions that only require you to *find* the correct answer within the given data. Your standard Science passage will include data in one of several classic forms: tables, bar graphs, and line graphs. A typical W1 question will indicate what data item to go to, and getting the correct answer to such a question is likely only a matter of locating what a given graph, chart, or table will smoothly reveal.

W1 questions should not feel in any way challenging. W1 questions should take less than a minute. W1 questions are scattered throughout a given Science section, and one of your first priorities will be to learn to recognize them.

You can be assured that by reading through LTSA and by doing your QOTW, you will comfortably be able to identify W1 questions!

▶ All Text (AT)

One of the Science passages will be what we call the All Text passage. This passage has always had 7 total questions. It should typically be very easy to identify as it will typically not have the traditional data that goes along with a standard Science passage.

Another way to identify the AT passage is that it should include the opinions of more than one person, and these people should be clearly labeled and separated. For instance, in your typical AT passage, you will see that there are opinions from *Scientist 1* and *Scientist 2*. A different AT might have opinions from *Student 1, Student 2,* and *Student 3*.

As we are only now mapping out your core roadmap, let us simply establish is that the first thing you will do with the AT when you see it on test day is SKIP the whole passage. You will most certainly come back and attack it, but you will not likely do so when you initially encounter it.

▶ Wave 2 (W2)

A simple initial way to characterize what Wave 2 questions are is to say that they are NOT questions that fit either of the first two categories that we mapped out, W1 and AT.

W2 questions are questions that are part of standard passages that you will initially skip. Why might you skip them? We will go into more detail later, but for now, let's simply acknowledge that you are going to skip them because they are more complex than W1 questions.

W2 questions might require you to understand what is happening within a given experiment, versus what a W1 question requires of you, which often is simply to see precisely what a given table might very clearly indicate.

W2 questions are questions that we have every intention of coming back to, and so skipping them initially is certainly not a defeat. The idea is to create incredibly positive momentum by initially knocking out all of the W1 questions and leaving questions that pose some degree of risk for later.

▶ Random Guessing (RG)

For the vast, VAST majority of students taking the ACT properly, there should be some questions that they never feel comfortable figuring out. Therefore, there are some questions on the day of your real exam that you will likely just put a random answer for. This is also far from a defeat! Understanding that you can, and should, simply guess on some questions is an important tactical aspect of crushing the ACT.

By the time you make it to the end of this portion of the book, you will have a clear sense of just how many questions you could potentially consider acceptable RGs in order for you to achieve specific score goals.

▶ Wave 3 (W3)

Just as I mentioned previously that a vast majority of students will have a chunk of questions fall into the RG category, the vast majority of students will also never need to consider the existence of Wave 3 questions.

W3 questions are questions that you initially skipped past (W2s), and when you came back to them, they were still clearly more complex than nearly any other question within the whole Science section. W3 questions will actually get skipped a second time.

Let me know acknowledge that really only students who are trying to score 34 or higher in Science will ever really need to acknowledge W3 questions. So if you already know that that is not a target score you will likely aim for, you can go ahead and skip to the next part of this portion of the book.

For those of you who are aspiring to hit a 34 or higher, a key aspect of actually doing so will simply be acknowledging what W3 questions are. We will talk more later about precisely you will need to do with them. But for now, I can assure you that once you recognize W3 questions, you will not even need to actually get all of them correct to achieve your score goal.

▶ *The Road to 27*

Ok, now that we have set up some clear markers and terms to reference, let's put some of this together and map out a plan that should consistently lead to scoring at least a 27 in Science. (For those of you targeting a score higher than 27, you'll see your roads mapped out in the *Targets & Expectations* portion of this part of the book.)

It is exceptionally likely that the very first block of Science questions, which the ACT will separately label as "Passage I", will be a standard passage that contains a chart, or a table, or some sort of normal looking graph. This passage will contain W1 questions, as basically every standard passage does. Your job on the day of the test is to obliterate those W1 questions, and while you are doing so, you are skipping other questions to potentially do during Wave 2.

Let's imagine that Passage I had six total questions. If that was the case, it is entirely possible that three of them would end up being W1s and three of them would end up being skipped for later. After completing all of the W1s, it is time to move to the next passage.

Let's now imagine that Passage II is another standard Science passage with a bar graph and a table. There will be W1 questions within this passage as well. Find them, do them, skip anything that seems more complicated, and build the positive momentum that you are very much capable of building my friend.

Now let's imagine that Passage III is the AT. Skip it. You will be doing it later. You'll be doing it fairly soon, by the way, but you will NOT be doing it when you first come across it.

Your mission right now is clear: find and complete all W1 questions first.

How will you know when you have completed this mission? You will know because you will have made it to the final question in the section, #40. On the road to that final question, you will have assertively skipped around, decisively seeking out only the W1 questions.

▶ *CheckPoint #1 - At the end of Wave 1, there is a good chance that you will have completed around 15 questions. All 15 of these questions should be correct, since you were only doing W1 questions, and those questions are supposed to be ones that are near impossible to get wrong, since nearly all of them should be questions that do NOT require any science knowledge.*

Now that Wave 1 is complete, you are going to go back to the AT passage. Completing the AT passage, and its seven questions is your second order of business. We will soon be talking about how to do the AT passage. For now, we are simply establishing that it comes second.

If you are specifically on the Road to 27, some good news to now get is that in order to achieve the really great score of 27, you can afford to feel confused by two of the seven questions within the AT passage. This is not to say that you will be confused by two of the questions; there is simply room for you not to love all seven questions.

▶ *CheckPoint #2 - You will now have completed basically half of the section, and it is likely that less than half of the time has gone by. You should likely have at least 20 questions correct (the 15 W1s and at least 5 of the ATs).*

With the AT passage complete, it is time to begin Wave 2. Doing so is super simple! You are just going to back to the very first question that you initially skipped, which should likely be within Passage I.

Your mission now is to figure out *some* of these W2 questions. As you'll see as your ACT journey continues, there will be some very straightforward W2 questions. These were questions that still should have been initially skipped for a variety of reasons, but when you come back to them during this Wave 2, you are able to comfortably get a good number of them.

To crunch some numbers, if you did do 15 W1s, and we know that there are always 7 ATs, then there would be 22 potential W2 questions. To successfully complete your mission within Wave 2, unbelievably, you only need to get about half of these potential 22 correct! So to be crystal clear, as you going through these questions, it really can be that you get one and then you re-skip one.

▶ *CheckPoint #3 - You should now have about 30 questions correct! You already had the 15 W1s and 5 ATs. Add to them, let's say, 10 W2s, and we are at 30 correct. At this point, time might be winding down in the section.*

And so this brings us to the RG stage of your road. Any questions that you did not feel comfortable with during Wave 2 still need to at least be guessed on, since there is no penalty for getting any questions wrong. Imagining that you were able to get 10 of the potential 18 W2 questions, there would be 8 RGs. Given that Science questions have four answer options, probability dictates that random guessing should give you at least 2 more correct answers.

▶ *Your Final Destination*

So tallying it all up my friend, you could complete the Science section and smoothly end up with 32 total correct answers. On nearly every ACT, this should translate to at least a score of 27. On quite a few exams, getting 32 would end up equating to a 28, and possibly even a 29.

In case it helps to see it, your *Road to 27* included:

- 15 Wave 1 questions correct
- 5   All Text questions correct
- 10 Wave 2 questions correct
- 2   Random Guesses correct

We have a lot more to talk about, but this should give you a good overall sense of how you are going to control things on the day of your exam.

The AT Passage

We do need to separately discuss how to actually approach the AT passage, beyond the strategy of initially skipping past it.

So let's imagine that Wave 1 is complete. You have made it to question #40, and you have confidently crushed more than a dozen questions. Now it's time to make your way back to the AT passage.

As we have briefly discussed, the AT will have more than one person's opinion, and these opinions will be clearly separated. Prior to the start of these opinions, which could be labeled *Scientist A, Scientist B*, etc., there is written information that we can simply refer to as the setup information.

Now, eventually Science Mantra #2 will be burned into your head forever. For now, let's reiterate that that mantra states to not read anything until it is necessary. The idea behind this is straightforward: there are many, many Science questions that can be very effectively answered without ever reading the written blurbs that go along with the data that is found within standard Science passages.

However, given that the AT will typically be entirely text, we do need to break from Mantra #2 when we are dealing with this particular passage. So, from the start of doing the AT passage, you will indeed need to flat out read everything. But you are not going to read everything in the same manner.

You will certainly begin by reading the setup information that is at the start of the AT. But while you are reading this information, which is sometimes very short, sometimes mildly lengthy, you are NOT going to be trying to really understand much. If you are able to understand what you are reading, fantastic! But if you are not really understanding what you are reading within the setup information, it's equally cool. You want to read the setup info so that you have a sense of what you are about to deal with, but typically an actual understanding of that material is not essential when it comes to actually answering the seven AT questions.

What really matters is what comes next, which is when you read through the different opinions of the listed people. Now is when you will start to physically mark up what each person is talking about. This is not to be confused with what we do in Reading when we write notes. So you are NOT writing things down as you are reading through each person's opinion. You are going to potentially underline, circle, box, and draw arrows.

What are you going to be looking for to mark up?

The primary things you are looking for are differences and similarities between the various given opinions. You are also looking for key words that might be significant to what a given person might be stating. The reason you are doing this is because many of the seven questions to follow will be tied to the differences and similarities between the different people.

Before I give you some examples of the types of things you might circle and box out, let me be clear that as you are marking things up, you do not need to actually be understanding everything that you are reading. Believe it or not, it will very likely be enough to find some differences and similarities. Actually understanding what they mean or what they are is very likely secondary.

So what might you mark up?

Some things will naturally stand out to you, such as numbers or something that was *italicized*. Though these things naturally stand out a bit already, I would go ahead and circle them or box them out, so that they stand out even more.

I would definitely circle specific elements that get mentioned, as one person might mention one element, while the other person mentions a different one. So I would circle FE if one person was talking about iron. And in another person's opinion, I would circle the CO if that person was mentioning carbon monoxide. The awesome thing is that I don't even need to know what these chemical symbols mean! I simply need to know that one person was talking about one thing, while the other was talking about another thing.

Ok, we are going to do more work together in regards to marking things up. So for now, let me leave things at this. And wonderfully, what I can most assuredly tell you is that once you get into even a decent rhythm with marking up the AT passage, quite a few questions will fall right into your lap once you get to them.

Things You MUST Memorize

Ok, you're starting to get used to things, right?

To be successful on a rigorous exam like the ACT, there are some things that you flat out need to memorize. As I say live all the time to student audiences, if you are not going to memorize what's about to follow, then why are you even taking the test?!

Let's get to it my friend.

1) W.H.E.A.R.

This is an acronym for five key words, words that will tell you immediately that a question is NOT a Wave 1 question.

>   Why   How   Explain   Assume   Reason

Each of these words hints at the fact that a question is extremely likely to be more involved than a W1 question is supposed to be. For instance, if I need to *explain* something, I likely need to understand at least some of the details of the given experiment. If I need to understand some of the details of the given experiment, then I likely need to do more than simply go straight to a data table of a bar graph.

So basically, if you see any of these five buzz words, immediately skip the question and save it for Wave 2.

A final comment to make is that variations of these words will also signal for you to skip a given question and not include it in Wave 1. So if you see the word "explanation" or "assumption", it is certainly the same as seeing "explain" or "assume"

2) Independent Variables

Let's not get technical, as we basically never do. And let's make things as simple as possible, as we basically always do.

Independent variables are things within the experiment that the person doing the experiment CHANGES.

So, for instance, within a given experiment, the person conducting the experiment might be testing how different temperatures affect whatever is being tested. Accordingly, the experimenter *changes* the temperature by five degrees and monitors what happens. Given this, the temperature would be considered an *independent variable*.

One final comment to make about independent variables is that if you are given numeric data, then independent variables are typically revealed by numbers that increase or decrease in a very clear and steady manner.

So if the mass of the amount of salt involved within a given experiment went from 0 grams to 5 grams to 10 grams to 15 grams, it would basically definitely be true that the amount of salt was an independent variable. These steady increases should fit nicely with the idea that independent variables are things that the experimenter *changes*, which is why the changes would be very consciously controlled.

3) Dependent Variables

Dependent variables are things within the experiment that the person doing the experiment MEASURES.

So, for instance, within a given experiment, the person conducting the experiment might be testing how different temperatures affects the growth of a certain species of plant. Accordingly, the experimenter *measures* the height of the plant at every noted temperature. Given this, the height would be considered a *dependent variable*.

You will not be surprised now to read that if you are given numeric data, then dependent variables are typically revealed by numbers that increase or decrease in a manner that is NOT steady.

So if the height of a given plant was 11.5 at a certain temperature and then 13.6 at a different temperature and then 15.2 at yet another temperature, it would basically definitely be true that the height is indeed a dependent variable. These non-steady values should fit nicely with the idea that dependent variables are things that the experimenter *measures*, which is why the values cannot be consciously controlled to be nice, pretty numbers.

4) A Control

With the last of the definitions we need to hit, let's continue to keep things simple.

The *control* of an experiment can be thought of the thing within the experiment that is LEFT ALONE.

A second way to think of what a control is is to think of it as the thing that GETS NOTHING.

So, for instance, if within a given experiment, there were a series of pots that were being given fertilizer in order to test the affect of the fertilized, the *control* would be the pot that got no fertilizer. It's the pot that was left alone.

This is why if within a given Science passage, you were given numeric data, a control could be revealed by the presence of a zero(0).

5. The PH Scale

The PH scale goes up to 14.

A PH of 7 means the thing is NEUTRAL.

When the PH is BELOW 7, then the thing is an ACID. The lower the number, the more acidic the thing is.

When the PH is ABOVE 7, then the thing is a BASE. The higher the number, the more basic the thing is.

Ok that's it. It hurts my brain to write anything more complicated than calling these things "things". Happily, I can still crush the Science and get a 36 and have this absurdly rudimentary knowledge of science. And with enough time and experience, there is very little (if anything) that I can do that you couldn't train to do as well my friend.

6. No Trap Answers

Basically, what I want to establish with this last "Must" point is that any answer could be the correct answer to a Science question.

To give you a point of contrast, within the Math sections of a variety of standardized tests, an answer option that said that the answer "cannot be determined" is basically never correct. Such an answer has been a classic trap answer used quite a few times in the past.

But within the Science section of the ACT, any answer option could be correct. Depending on the data that is given to you, a situation within a Science question may not be possible to determine. And so any answer, even one that stated that something "cannot be determined" could be the correct answer to a Science question on test day.

Things You Should TRY to Memorize

To get to a 27 in Science, you could likely get away with skipping this part of this section of the book.

If you are trying to push past a 27, then you should likely *try* to memorize what's here, hence the title of this portion of the book. Let's get to it, shall we?

1. Reactants & Products

Reactants are the items on the LEFT side of a given equation.

Products are the items on the RIGHT side of a given equation.

So if a given Science passage says that something *reacts* with oxygen, then both the oxygen and what that something is should be on the LEFT side of the given equation.

2. PV:T

The "P" stands for *pressure*, and the "V" stands for *volume*, while the "T" stands for *temperature*.

What you need to potentially memorize is that pressure(P) and volume(V) are *inversely* related. If one of them goes up, the other goes down. If one of them increases, the other decreases. You can memorize this idea by acknowledging that the items on the same side vary inversely.

The items on opposite sides are *directly* related. So if pressure(P) goes up, then temperature(T) goes up. If volume(V) goes down, then temperature(T) goes down.

3. Odd Man Out Theory

The idea is fairly straightforward: there may be something within a question that separates one of the choices from the other three. When this happens, it is exceptionally likely that the correct answer is the one that stands alone.

The rationale behind this idea is also straightforward: if there is something that lumps the other three answer options together, how could you choose between them. Therefore, the correct answer must be the option that stands alone.

If we are lucky, you will be able to use this theory once or twice on a given exam.

Things You CHOOSE to Memorize

Many students should make the proper choice of ignoring what's within this portion of the exam.

What's here is a combination of oddball material and facts that are not very likely to appear on any given exam.

That said, if the mission is to absolutely obliterate the Science portion of the exam, which means scoring a 34 or higher, then you know what you need to do. So what are you waiting for?! Start memorizing!

1 Drag Force

Even though we getting into some rather nerdy material, that doesn't change the fact that I am going to keep things super simple.

And so, very simply *drag force* will make something slower.

So if there was MORE drag force, then the speed of a given something would be less. And conversely, if there was LESS drag force, then the speed of a given something would be more.

2 Potential Energy

The *potential energy* of something is the greatest BEFORE it starts to move.

Once it starts moving, the energy is a different kind of energy.

What?! Were you expecting more? When we're dealing with ACT Science, we are keeping things as simple as possible my friend!

Six Specialty Questions

Getting super comfortable with the various ways you are getting tested within the Science section of the ACT is kind of the whole point.

You are hopefully getting very comfortable (and maybe even excited) with the idea that knocking out this part of the exam is NOT really at all about just being smart or "good" at science.

We are cultivating a unique skill, and the next phase of how we need to do so is by dissecting these fairly important specialty questions. So let's get to it, shall we?

1 Split Questions (SQ)

Potential Frequency:

It would seem like you can anticipate seeing this type of question on the day of your exam quite a bit, meaning at least a half dozen times.

Priority Level:

Given how frequently this type of question will appear on the test day, you need to have at least a solid handle on it. And what's about to follow is nothing heavy duty either, so it probably makes sense to master what we're about to discuss.

Fundamental Idea/Approach:

When you encounter an SQ, it will eventually be very obvious. Split Questions have answer options that are clearly split, and they basically always split in two different ways. For instance, two of the answer options may start with "Gas A" and two of the answer options may start with "Gas B". Or, two of the options will begin with the word "increasing", while two of the other options will begin with the word "decreasing".

Later, within the options, there will almost definitely be a second split. So one of the answers that started with "increasing", then later says "increase", while the other answer that started with "increasing", then later says "decrease". There is a wide variety of ways that the options could split within SQs, but you can trust me that it will become very manageable for you to notice when you are dealing with an SQ.

The great thing about SQs is that pretty much all of them will have two answer options that can fairly quickly be eliminated because they clearly violate the data provided within the passage.

For example, within an SQ that splits from the beginning via "increasing" and "decreasing", there is a very strong chance that the data within the passage will clearly indicate whether whatever is being discusses is indeed increasing or decreasing. And so, without any major work, two answer options will likely be eliminated within a typical SQ.

For most students, *Random Guessing*(RG) is an essential part of the overall game plan. It is a part of the game plan even when a student is hoping to score past 30. It should just now be clear that SQs should basically never be a RG, as at the least, two choices should likely be eliminated.

After those initial two options are knocked out, if you are really uncertain as to how to decide between the remaining options, then it certainly makes sense to decisively select one of the choices and move on.

The Next Level:

A theme that will establish itself naturally within this part of the test is that you cannot rush the way you arrive at correct answers. The information involved within Science passages tends to get very nitpicky, and therefore, very easy to misread.

So with SQs in particular, because the initial decision you make will hopefully successfully knock out two wrong answers, take your time to be sure that you are processing the information correctly and getting rid of the right two options.

Final Comment:

As mentioned earlier, the classic SQ splits in two ways. Depending on the question, one of the way in which a given SQ splits may be a touch simpler to process than the other. So don't be rigid.

If you use how the answers seem to split toward the beginning, or if you use how the answers seem to split later within each option, either way, you will have hopefully efficiently knocked out two wrong answers.

And as a final, final comment, let's acknowledge that how you determine the correct final answer was not really the point of this whole discussion. That final decision will likely be super context specific. And happily, how you make that final decision will often not require any super human ability.

The main point of this discussion on SQs was to drive home the point that even a big, bulky, intimidating SQ is one that should at least allow you to be taking a great guess between two remaining options.

❷ Column Questions (CQ)

Potential Frequency:

It would seem like you can anticipate seeing this type of question on the day of your exam at least two or three times, and hopefully, many more times.

Priority Level:

I said "hopefully" in the previous paragraph because CQs tend to be very, very manageable questions. We are looking to flat out crush all of them that we are fortunate enough to get on test day.

Fundamental Idea/Approach:

CQs are immediately recognizable. As is often the case with how I name things within LTSA, I wasn't going for anything creative. Column Questions are called Column Questions because the answer options have columns.

And the reason that I wanted to single out these questions is because I wanted you to know that they are friends. CQs should typically be exceptionally straightforward.

CQs also have a connection to SQs in that you can pretty much always efficiently get rid of two of the answer options. For instance, within one column, you might notice that two of the answer options give you one value, let's say 13. Within that same column, two other answer options will give you a different value, let's say 14. Based on the data that the given question is asking you to reference, it should be fairly clear whether the correct answer includes a 13 or a 14, and just like that two options are eliminated.

Within a CQ, there could be two or three different columns of information. And so, with two options eliminated via one of the columns, it should likely only being a matter of referencing a different column to determine the correct final answer.

Final Comment:

There's kind of no "Next Level" or really even much of a final comment to make here my friend.

CQs are friends. We are hoping to see a bunch of them on test day, because odds are you will steam roll all of them. If there are only two or three, well then, we'll be thankful for at least those two or three.

On that positive note, let's head into the next question type.

③ Extrapolation Questions (EQ)

Potential Frequency:

It would seem like you can anticipate seeing this type of question at least two or three times on the day of your exam.

Priority Level:

I'm putting this question type next, because you kind of need to just flat out pick this item up. Happily, there is also nothing heavy duty to pick up.

Fundamental Idea/Approach:

The idea here is pretty straightforward. Most of the passages give you some data, as you may already be getting very accustomed to. That data, as you may also be getting accustomed to, can be in the form of a data table, a bar graph, a line graph, etc. Within each of the previously mentioned forms of data, it is possible to ask an Extrapolation Question.

Basically, what an EQ is asking you to do is extend the given data in a logical way. The way the data could extend could be in any natural manner.

For instance, let's say that in a given trial labeled "Trial 1", the measurement for the salt content was 20. And then in Trial 2, the measurement was 25, and then in Trial 3, the measurement was 30. A classic EQ could ask you to predict what would happen if there was a Trial 4.

So like basically all of Science, there's no trick here. You are supposed to be thinking that in this hypothetical case, the measurement for Trial 4 would be 35.

The Next Level:

If a given EQ is tied to a line graph, it would be silly not to adhere to Mantra #4: *Mark It Up*. Physically drawing an extension to whatever line is being referenced by the question should not only make logical sense, but it also should be resonating with the test-taking side of your persona that we are cultivating!

If a given EQ is tied to a data table, it would be a great test-taking move to circle or box out the last set of data that you are supposed to be extrapolating from.

Final Comment:

Don't lose sight of the fact that a given EQ could be asking you to determine what would happen from either natural direction. So as is kind of always the case when it comes to Science as a whole, don't rush anything. As you'll be reading later when we get to our Mediations for this part of the exam, you can really only go as fast as you can go. Your goal is not to be fast, but to be accurate.

4. In-Between Questions (IB)

Potential Frequency:

You should likely see at least one of these on the day of your exam, but it is not impossible for there to actually be none.

Priority Level:

Given that it is possible that you might not see an IB on test day, it would seem like this question type should have the lowest priority. However, given its similarities to the EQ, we're discussing it next. And you should likely just pick this one up as well.

Fundamental Idea/Approach:

Why this type of question is referred to as an In-Between will be very obvious. No surprise, right?

Let's imagine that you are shown that for a given sample of whatever, at 10 degrees, the measurement was 80. And then you are shown that at 20 degrees, the measurement was 70. A classic IB would now ask you to determine what the measurement would likely be at 15 degrees.

At this stage in your preparation, you are understanding that, yet again, there are no tricks here. The correct answer is almost definitely going to be 75.

The Next Level

Keep marking things up!

I personally like to circle things when I am dealing with an IB. My circles make it super clear which values I need to be in-between. And my circles make it basically impossible for me to misread something or make any type of mistake.

Ok, I think we're ready to just move on now my friend.

5 Science-Sense Questions (SS)

Potential Frequency:

It would seem like you can anticipate seeing this type of question on the day of your exam a very solid number of times, like say around a half dozen or so.

Priority Level:

Ok, so actually, there really aren't any of the types of questions that don't have at least a solid degree of importance attached to them. There's only six types, and as you've already seen, there isn't that much to memorize within this portion of the test. And I am going to continue to acknowledge that nothing in what we're about to discuss is anything too heavy duty for you to pick up.

Fundamental Idea/Approach:

The basic idea of this type of question is that some degree of *science-sense* is going to be necessary for you to get the question correct.

Now before you get nervous about that comment, let me remind you that I am brutally uncomfortable with science in general. But even as brutal as I naturally am with science, even I possess some degree of what I have gotten to calling science-sense. I think we should go straight to an example.

A SS question might ask you to figure out why a certain type of material was used involving an experiment in which bacteria growth was being monitored. It wouldn't take any keen awareness of science to understand why a correct answer would include the idea that that type of material allows for bacteria to be grown on it. Believe it or not, in such a question, one of the wrong answer options would say something like that type of material does NOT allow bacteria to be grown on it.

But if the purpose of the experiment is to see how bacteria might grow, then it only makes sense (hence the name of this question type) that the material used within the experiment allows for bacteria to grow on it.

Ok, nothing so bad right? And you understand why this question is called what it's called? If so, things are shaping up nicely my friend, very nicely.

The Next Level:

You might have noticed that I didn't talk about how to recognize SSs like I usually do within the "Idea/Approach" portion of this discussion.

The reason for not doing so is kind of because there is nothing to really discuss. This is actually pretty much a good thing, because it means that you are not really going to need to consciously know that you are dealing with an SS in order to effectively deal with it. Your ingrained science-sense is simply going to take control of the situation and very naturally lead you to the correct answer.

As an example, if a different Science question asked you about a "metal", I don't imagine that we need to review which materials are metals and which ones are not in order for you to be properly prepared. If I need to remind you that iron is a metal, for instance, there's kind of no hope for you in the Science section of the ACT, the ACT itself, and probably even life.

Final Comment:

Ok, all joking aside from what I just said, there are some elements of your "science-sense" that we can cultivate.

For example, if you saw a graph that was a flat horizontal line, you could be trained to acknowledge that such a line would represent a situation in which nothing was changing. (If this is a comment that seems overly simple or oddly strange, I would not be concerned.)

A different SS might ask you to simply acknowledge that negative temperatures are cold. Sometimes comments like that are so obvious that within a given Science question, you could overcomplicate the situation unless we had discussed, as we doing now, that you shouldn't overcomplicate the situation.

In closing, also keeping our most important Science Mantra in mind, Mantra #1: *Not Trying to Trick You*, you are going to learn to trust your science-sense the more you use it. In most cases, when there's more of something, it really is because something is increasing. When a graph is labeled with certain labels, those labels really are just trying to reveal to you what the given experiment is testing.

I am thinking that this science-sense conversation is making sense. If it's not, you need to let me know somehow. But if it is, then it is time to head to our final question type.

6 *Fact Questions (FQ)*

Potential Frequency:

It seems like it is going to fluctuate from test to test in regards to how many of these you will see. There will definitely be at least one or two, but there could be as many as around a half dozen.

Priority Level:

There is a bit of fluctuation here as well. Depending on what fact might be getting tested, you should definitely get a given FQ. But a different FQ could actually be the least important question within the entire section. As you read on, you'll very much understand these comments.

Fundamental Idea/Approach:

One way that you will know that you are dealing with an FQ is because you will recognize something within either the question or answer options that you know that you already know/memorized. This could be something that you know because of a high school class. It could be something that you memorized from LTSA! Either way, some FQs will stand out when you encounter them.

We love this type of FQ, as it is one that you are nicely prepared for. So if a given question asked you to identify what is the "independent variable" within a given experiment, and that is a term that you had already memorized, you would be good to go.

If a different FQ asked you about "drag force", maybe you had memorized the simple articulation of that idea from LTSA. Or maybe, you already understood that concept because of your awesome high school teacher person. Either way, such a question should pose little resistance to you.

The Next Level:

But now we need to talk about the other side of the FQ spectrum. We need to discuss the possibility that you will encounter a question on test day that does require you to know a fact, but you do NOT know that fact. This is a circumstance, that even after all of these years that I've been immersed within the ACT, I still need to anticipate finding myself within.

To give you a clear example, on one given exam, a question asked about the kinetic theory of gases. My knowledge of that theory back then was zero. My knowledge of that theory at this exact moment is still zero. Knowing that my knowledge was and probably forever will be zero when it comes to that theory, I simply put a random guess and moved on. I need you ready to do the same thing my friend.

We're not far from talking about Targets & Expectations for Science. To give you a sneak peek: you don't even need to get all 40 questions to always get a perfect 36. So even on that day when I was "beaten" by that question, I still *earned* a 36 in Science.

If you're wondering by the way whether there was anything within the passage that gave any hint regarding what the kinetic theory of gases actually was, I can tell you there wasn't. The question definitely flat out required us that day to already just know. And I can tell you that I actually didn't even bother to check if there was anything within the setup information that mentioned that theory. There will likely come a time, as you accumulate the necessary experience you happen to require to make your particular ACT dream materialize naturally, when you will develop a bit of a sixth sense. With that level of experience under your belt, if you sense that you are dealing with an FQ, I suspect you will be correct.

Final Comment:

It is possible that a given FQ would require you to do a mini-calculation. I use "mini" in that word because any calculation that you would need to do within the Science section of the test would be light work for sure.

You are not permitted to use a calculator during the Science section of the test. Knowing this, the ACT isn't trying to torment you with any complex calculation. In fact, if you ever think that you are stumped by a question because you feel the need to use a calculator, it likely means you are misinterpreting what the question is actually asking you to do.

The kind of calculation you might need to perform within an actual FQ would be something like 5 times 20, or something like what's 50% of 80.

On that note, let's close out this discussion then by acknowledging what I was talking about earlier. There are going to be some FQs that are super straightforward and simple for you because you flat out know the fact that is being tested.

On the other hand, you could get a question that asks you about a fact that you could not have anticipated being asked about. There are FQs, like my friend the kinetic theory of gases question, that presented the need to know a very specific fact, but that fact was only tested that one time, that one day.

The facts that could be tested more regularly are here within the "MUST", "TRY", and "CHOOSE" portions of this part of the book. And so with pride, I tell you that I will never, Never, NEVER learn what the kinetic theory of gases is. If you know, then cool, but don't tell me, because it's never going to be necessary for me to know in order to crush the ACT. And if you don't know, then cool, and I hope you feel zero urge to google what it is!

Seven Science Meditations

1 Scan, Don't Read

We are aiming to be maximally efficient on test day. Accordingly, there are moments when you should be *scanning*, not reading.

For instance, a particular question could mention something about how a new hypothetical situation is 10 degrees colder than what was originally the case. So, instead of passively reading through all of the initial setup information that may happen to be included within a given passage, I could alternatively very actively scan the setup information for a number, specifically a number tied to a temperature.

Assuming I found such a number, there is an exceptionally good chance that it is the only number tied to a temperature within the passage, so using it to help me answer a given question should be very well justified.

2 Ignore Baseline Material

Within certain questions, there is material that I have grown accustomed to calling *baseline material* that you want to learn to ignore. This baseline material is material that is connected to the Science passage as a whole, but it isn't directly tied to the particular question that we are trying to answer.

For instance, a given question might mention that an experiment was conducted at a temperature of 25 degrees Celsius or a 1 atmosphere of pressure. These conditions were likely the conditions that were indeed mentioned within the setup of the experiment. But these conditions also might not have anything to do with the particular question we are tackling. That question could simply be asking you to see what Figure 1 is showing.

And so, it will likely become important for you to selectively ignore certain material that does not have any direct impact on answering given questions.

3. The Axes Matter

Don't take for granted how the axes of a particular graph might be labeled. Doing so definitely leads to classic mistakes.

For instance, on a specific graph, both the left AND the right sides might have separate labels. One side could correspond to one set of data and the other side could correspond to another set of data.

As a second example, if there were two graphs, do not take for granted that their axes are the same. One could be scaled with completely different numbers or units than the other.

4. Eliminate As You Can

A major goal of ours within Science is to be as efficient as possible, to take the path of least resistance. Along those lines, there will likely be a question or two in which we can streamline the amount of work we actually need to do.

For example, a specific question could ask us which of four experiments are supported by new information supplied by the specific question. If we realized that "Experiment 1" definitely was not supported by the new information, then any answer option that includes Experiment 1 can be crossed out. This might leave us with only two options left, one of which include "Experiment 2" and one of which that doesn't.

This means that all we may have left to really do is make a decision on Experiment 2. The fact that some of the answer options might mention "Experiment 3" or "Experiment 4" may not even matter.

5. Oddball Passages are W2s

It is very likely that all of the Science passages other than the AT Passage will be what we can refer to as *standard* passages. As defined earlier within this portion of the book, standard passages are ones that contain data in standard forms, which include bar graphs, numeric tables, and line graphs.

Every so often, though, the ACT presents us with an "oddball" passage. This is NOT an AT, because there is data, and very simply because it's just not an AT. (By the time you take your real exam, spotting the AT will likely be super simple.) An "oddball" passage might have very unconventional figures or data presented in a very unique manner.

At some point, it will not likely be difficult for you at all to spot an oddball passage. What I need to you to know from a strategic standpoint is that it should make perfect sense to leave an oddball passage for the start of Wave 2.

6. Know If You're Beat

One of my greatest skills is being able to immediately identify when I am just completely mystified by a particular question. As you will read at the end of the section, even if you were trying to score a perfect 36, there is a solid chance that you could afford to have absolutely no idea how to do a given question.

The skill that I would love to see you cultivate is to know if you happen to be beat and very decisively get the hell out and devote your time and effort to other questions that actually warrant your time and effort.

7. You Can't Go Faster Than You Can Go

Like we also spoke about within one of the Reading Meditations, you can't really rush things and hope to do well on test day.

For instance, if you read a given question too quickly and then misinterpret what you need to do, then you're dead in the water to begin with. Even worse actually, you spend time working on a question only to have that time be a complete waste, because you are only getting a wrong answer anyway!

Ultimately, when it really comes down to it, within Science in particular, you can't really go faster than you can go. The time it takes you to find the correct answer is the time it takes you. Getting through the questions "faster" isn't about reading faster. It is about being more efficient with what you are doing. And happily, cultivating some speed within the Science section will also be a natural byproduct of getting more and more accustomed to the specific nuances of the section itself.

Targets & Expectations

So maybe now you understand why I said earlier that I really believe that every dedicated student can *earn* a Science score of at least 27.

Beating this part of the test is NOT easy. I never say that really any aspect of the ACT is easy. But there is a blueprint that you can follow that can lead you to the score that you need. And actually, let's address a happy thing as we head into some final numbers.

Just because I know you can get a 27, that doesn't mean you personally *need* one. If the dream that you are trying to make more than just a dream doesn't require you to get a 27, then I think it's amazing that you know. Accordingly, read past some of the categories that are about to be mentioned.

Different dreams for different students. This is a happy thing my friend. A very happy thing.

▶ 34 to 36

So we need to first acknowledge the fluctuations that most certainly do exist within the scoring of the Science section. On some exams, you could miss a question and still score a perfect 36. On other exam, if you miss one question, your score here is a 34. I know that seems crazy and unfair, but it is what it is my friend, so let's just discuss what practically matters.

What practically matters is that to score within this zone, you can typically afford to miss 2 questions. And really the best way to incorporate that idea into a clear game plan is to do what I certainly do myself, which is to realize that there could be up to 4 questions that I initially find really, really uncomfortable.

Imagine a scenario in which you have completed Wave 1. You also felt confident that you got six out of the seven ATs. This could mean that coming out of Wave 2, there could be three questions that still make you uncomfortable and that you opted to come back to for your Wave 3.

Let's further imagine that you only have those three questions left to do when the proctor calls outs that there are five minutes left. The best mentality to now have is to realize that within the remaining five minutes, if you could even confidently figure out one or two of these last remaining questions, you should be able to score within this range.

Not knowing the kinetic theory of gases didn't stop me from getting a perfect 36. It's largely because I didn't let not knowing it bother me.

▶ *31 to 33*

To score within this range, you should be thinking that you could miss between 3 to 5 questions. So what does this practically mean?

Well you are going to crush Wave 1, because we all crush Wave 1. When you get to the AT passage, it would be really wonderful if you could confidently get six of the seven questions, but it would not be a deal breaking disaster if you only felt great about five of them.

And then, I would love it if you realized that there could be up to at least a half dozen questions that you saved for Wave 3. Of those questions, you would need to figure out about half, but that is likely something that you could do if you weren't obsessed with trying to figure them all out.

By the time the proctor alerts you to the fact that there are five minutes left, you should be in Wave 3, and you should be feeling zero pressure to actually figure out whatever questions you have left. Random guessing on at least two or three questions will not be a problem.

▶ *28 to 30*

Not sure if you have read either of the other categories, but if you did, then it's pretty simple what can be said here. We can expand your amount of leeway within this part of the test!

You can generally miss at least 6 or 7 questions and still score within this range. So this means that after you dominate Wave 1, it could definitely be the case that you only needed to get five of the seven AT questions. From here, coming out of Wave 2, there could easily be around ten questions that you still haven't gotten. Of those ten questions, if you could get half of them, you should find yourself scoring within this range.

So we're talking about let's say 14 W1s, 5 ATs, and 9 W2s that you've already crushed. With ten questions left and probably a good amount of time still left on the clock, you could calmly pull off five more correct answers. And actually, because you're so calm, I can easily see you getting even more...

▶ *27*

There's like a whole road to this score that we already mapped out remember. Yeah, so like go back to that!

▶ 23 to 26

This is the final category that I am mapping out, because even if you think you are the worst science person in the history of the ACT, you can train yourself to score within this range. Reminder: I was awful at a lot of science in high school, and it's not like I've been generally reviewing science material since then.

Don't allow yourself to get overly frustrated with the fact that you aren't a natural at science. Get good at Science! (Hopefully, you get why one "science" is lowercase and the other is capitalized.)

To get to this range, there never needs to be a Wave 3. Questions that really confuse you, you can simply randomly guess on. You need to knock out Wave 1, and I know you can push yourself to pull out at least five of the seven ATs.

This potentially leaves us with a situation in which you have maybe around half of the section still left, and of that half, if you got half, then you would comfortably score within this range. It really can be that manageable.

Actually, I want to end on a bold note, since I started the Science section boldly as well. You shouldn't even really think about anything other than the process that I have mapped out for you, and I know you will score within this range.

Memorize core information, such as what makes W1 questions, W1 questions. Memorize what "MUST" be memorized. Study the question types. Read the Meditations. Maybe memorize some of what you should "TRY" to memorize. And that's really it my friend.

What I have written works. I know it works. Now you just need to make sure that you put in some work.

#OnlyHardWork

The Essay

The Essay

I'm not sure a single college exists out there that actually really does care about your essay (or Writing) score. The fact that it is "optional" kind of drives me crazy. Just tell me I need to do it! Or just build it into the exam and don't make it an "option".

The bottom line is this: because this silly Writing exercise exists, the safe thing to do is to take it at some point. Whether or not any college actually cares about your score, I do know that some colleges will state that they expected their applicants to have done it. And so, particularly, if I was a typical student who doesn't know exactly which colleges I plan on applying to, I would feel compelled to take the "optional" essay to ensure that nothing stupid happened down the road.

If a given college does actually care about your Writing score, how much might it care? Well, no one can likely say for sure, but I'm not sure why any rational college would care about an exercise that students take after already grinding through hours of a very rigorous test. If you didn't already know, the essay is administered after the four main parts of the ACT.

Ok, with all of that said, let's just get to the practicality of this matter. To be safe, you should take the ACT with Writing at some point in your test taking life. But I do think it is plausible to take it once, earn a good enough score and never take it again.

What is a good enough score? Well, the minimum score you can get is a 2. (So don't get excited if you took the Writing portion already and didn't get a 0.) The maximum score you can get is a 12. If you are not overly concerned about your essay score, but you are doing it just to be safe, AND you are not expecting to apply to some of the more high-powered schools in the nation, I think you can feel safe with an essay score of 7. And I would even go as far as to say that getting a 6 isn't likely going to be a dealbreaker when it comes to your future college applications.

However, if you are planning to apply to tougher schools, then I think you want a score that is 8 or higher. That said, I do not think any school, even the top schools, in the nation will care if you get a 9 versus a 10, or an 8 versus a 9. Colleges will most certainly care much more about your Composite score out of 36. Basically, what I am trying to tell those of you who are trying to realize some of the toughest college dreams out there is that if you score a 35 on the ACT and get an essay score of 9, not even the most selective of colleges will likely care at all that you scored a 9 versus something in the double digits.

So if you do get a satisfactory Writing score at any point, I think any future times you choose to sit for the ACT after having achieved that score, you could opt to take the test without the essay.

Ok, with everything that's been said so far, it's time for us to just get through some basics to ensure that you can earn at least a satisfactory score to potentially put this silliness behind you.

Things You MUST Memorize

❶ Longer is Better

You get four sides of paper for the essay. It just makes logical sense that the people who read your essay will need to reward students who end up generating more material. So if you can, I would highly advise trying to write at least three full pages. If you can write more, write more, but you should not feel like you need to fill up all four pages.

Something I like to do, partly because I don't have the best handwriting, is skip a line after every paragraph that I write. I think it makes my essay a bit easier to read for the person who reads it.

❷ Five Paragraph Minimum

So here's what basically going on with the essay. You're given a topic, one that is pretty much always something you'd already have a feel for. For instance, you could get a topic about school uniforms, about what books high school students should read, or about whether it is a good or bad thing that adults play video games.

You will then be given three different perspectives on the given topic. Your primary job is to clearly state your own perspective and to relate your opinion with the Perspectives that are given. Given what you are being tasked to do, it should be very simple to generate at least five paragraphs.

Start with an introduction of course, and end with a closing. (We'll actually talk more about both of those classic paragraphs.) Now, given that we are given three separate Perspectives, it should make sense why it should not be difficult for you to write at least three body paragraphs.

The most basic approach to the Writing exercise would be to have your second overall paragraph (also your first body paragraph) be a paragraph all about one of the three Perspectives, and particularly, one of the Perspectives that you don't agree with. In two or three sentences, you could recap what that particular Perspective was saying, and then in another two or three sentences you could explain why you don't agree with it or what issues you have with it.

Doing basically the same thing with a second Perspective that you don't agree with, you're now done with three paragraphs in total and comfortably on the second page of your essay. From here, if you wanted to take the easiest way out, you could have decided ahead of time to basically agree entirely with one of the Perspectives. If you're taking this approach, then your third body paragraph (fourth overall paragraph) would be commenting on the Perspective you agree with and obviously explaining why you agree. Add in your closing paragraph, and you have comfortably arrived at a five-paragraph essay.

Before we move on to the next point, let's acknowledge that it would be quite simple for you to extend your essay into a six-paragraph essay. Doing so would very possibly be essential if you were hoping to hit the full three-page length by the way. All you need to do is not outright agree with any of the three Perspectives. This way you have a separate body paragraph for commentary on each of the Perspectives, and then you can build a separate paragraph for your actual opinion.

What your actual opinion is by the way, really doesn't matter in any way. When I have written these silly essays in the past, I made my opinion something that never directly aligned with any of the given Perspectives. This way, I was always able to write more. And given that none of the topics that the ACT ever seems to give us are heavy duty topics, it should not be difficult for you to forge an opinion that does not directly match whatever was already given by the three established Perspectives.

❸ *Call Them Perspectives*

I assume that you noticed that I was regularly capitalizing the word "Perspectives". I wanted to almost subliminally establish for you to do so as well on the day of your exam.

The readers who are grading your exam will certainly be very familiar with the three Perspectives, so it only makes sense to directly reference them as they are labeled within the exam booklet. So when you are talking about Perspective One, definitely refer to it directly as "Perspective One".

As a final comment, the order in which you write about them certainly does not matter, so write about them in the order that you please.

❹ *Ok to Get Personal*

If you're a typical high school student, then you've likely been trained not to use the word "I" in any of your essays. This is something that you (and should) suspend for this exercise.

You're supposed to be be clearly stating your own perspective. Accordingly, it would be absolutely bizarre for you not to use the word "I".

5. Short Intro / Short Closing

Ok, our final point to make before we get into some nerdier material is that your introduction and your closing paragraphs can both be short. They could be as short as three sentences each, maybe even only two sentences each. The heart of the assignment is what you needed to do within the three (hopefully four) body paragraphs that you generated.

To make life nice and simple, all that your intro really must do is give two or three sentences that discusses what the overall topic happens to be. You do NOT need to already make it clear what your opinion is going to be. So I am outright telling you that a traditional thesis statement is NOT essential. I have gotten a perfect Writing score in the past without having a traditional thesis statement in my intro.

I basically never write a traditional thesis statement, by the way, because I am not even sure what position I am going to take before I start writing. I know I can write an intro that is made up mostly of just talking about the given topic. I also know that I am going to purposely not directly agree with any of the given Perspectives. Hence, I can start writing without having already formed my own opinion.

And in case you would find it helpful to know, my final sentence of my intro is usually something along the lines of, "Understandably, a variety of viewpoints exist in regards to this growing trend." The only thing I tend to vary is the last word or two, because I will change it based on whatever the topic happens to be. Maybe the topic deals with a current "trend", maybe it deals with a "debate", maybe it deals with a mild "controversy".

To talk briefly about the closing paragraph, I definitely do not do anything special. Having a sentence or two that classically mirrors some of what was mentioned in the intro is going to work. And by the time I am writing my closing, I would now have cemented what perspective is, so mentioning that one final time also makes sense. And quite frankly, knowing that a perfect Writing score isn't a concern for probably any college in existence, I am always quite content with keeping my closing short.

Things You CHOOSE to Memorize

Ok, we're skipping past the usual second tier of "TRY", because to be blunt, your Writing score just probably won't really matter. That is, as long as it's not horrendous. If you get an essay score of 3, I can't even begin to guess what went wrong. Was the topic on whether it's ok to wear t-shirts with controversial messages and you wrote about how you wish unicorns were real?

In any case, as long as you adhere to what was within the "MUST" portion, I am confident that you would comfortably score at least a 7 or an 8, and it is quite possible that following what was previously stated about the essay could lead to a double digit score.

So it would be quite understandable if you skipped over this last set of points about the essay and went right to the "Closing Remarks". But for those of you worry about dotting every "i" and crossing every "t", I got your back. Here's some more insight into the essay!

1. Pull It All Together

Ok, if you're still reading, then I know the most important point I can still make is about your potential second-to-last paragraph.

I went on an essay-taking binge once. I decided that I was going to keep signing up for the ACT with Writing until I got a perfect essay score. The first attempt in that essay-crazed cycle, I got close. So I made some adjustments and then my score actually went down. I made more adjustments, and my score went down again! Then I made the adjustment I'm about to talk about, and I finally scored a perfect score.

Part of the assignment is to "analyze the relationship between your perspective" and the given Perspectives. I had assumed that I was basically doing that already within my body paragraphs, so I kind of mentally checked off that box in my head as *mission complete*.

However, faced with the conundrum of why I was not achieving a perfect score, I made my second-to-last paragraph one day a kind of *pull it all together* kind of paragraph.

I started the paragraph by saying, "So, in relation to Perspective Two, I disagree the most because..." From there, I went on to compare my perspective to the other two Perspectives, varying my word choice. For instance, "I was closest in agreement to Perspective Three, since that author indicated..."

As I was writing this paragraph that afternoon, I felt as if what I was writing was almost too elementary. But I was tired of not getting perfect scores, and it was the only other thing I could think of that I was missing.

I cannot say with 100% certainty that this is a paragraph that every reader who is grading the essay requires, but I did end up scoring a perfect score that day on the essay. And because I did, I haven't taken the ACT with the essay since!

2 Nothing Academic

Ok, now we head into a series of small points, none of which I think are make or break ideas, especially since we are dealing with the least make or break aspect of the ACT. That said, if you're looking for a maximum level of insight into every nuance of the exam, well then, that's what I'm here to deliver.

Given the nature of the topics within the Writing exercise, I just wanted to relieve you from any unnatural pressure you might have been feeling to be in any way academic when it comes to what you write. If a given topic happens to be about whether it makes sense for an adult to collect toys, it doesn't seem salient to make a historical reference to Abraham Lincoln.

You most certainly need to back up the opinions that you give within your essay. You simply don't need to do so with academic information. Mostly because, it isn't really possible to do so anyway given the topics.

3 Speak Like Yourself

Picking up from the previous point, I also wanted to let you know that you shouldn't feel the need to drop in high-powered vocabulary words. That is unless, that's simply what you naturally do.

Having taught the SAT for quite a long time when that exam required people to know a lot of crazy words, I have naturally cultivated a strong vocabulary. I don't purposely use high-powered vocab words when I write standardized test essays, but given that they are a natural part of my vocabulary, I do use some from time to time. Using them has not seemed to affect my score, so again, I just wanted to let you know here that you can pretty much speak however it is that you speak.

4. *Citing "Statistics"*

I thought it was worth a brief moment to acknowledge that I am not a fan of using statistics within essay exercises like this. You'll notice that put the word "statistics" in quotes in the name of this point, because that's how I feel when I have read student essays in the past that used statistics.

Basically, I'm trying to say that any statistics used felt made up to me. As an example, when I polled some of my students recently, 93.7% of them agreed that the use of statistics felt disingenuous.

See what I mean? No?

Sorry, I was having a little fun, because I just wanted to spice things up a bit as I was writing about Writing tips. Bottom line: you're welcome to use statistics, but they are most certainly not something that seems to add much weight to the strength of an essay for an exercise like what you will face on the ACT.

Closing Remarks

Four Final Meditations

1. What Clock?

I acknowledge that the ACT was definitely constructed to make the time limits a challenge. Not everyone faces the same challenges on test day. For instance, most students would find the time limit a bigger challenge within the Reading section than within the English section.

That said, the ideal circumstance to find yourself in on test day is a circumstance in which you ignore the clock for the most part.

You may have noticed that there was no Math Meditation or Science Meditation in regards to checking the clock at all, whereas we did close out the English and Reading portions of this book by discussing a one-time time check. The rationale behind this is simple. When it comes to Math and Science, the clock should really be a zero factor. If you are skipping around the way that you should, and if you have developed an awareness of a variety of types of questions and facts, then your success within these sections should come down to what you know and the skill set you have cultivated. You can't really (and really definitely shouldn't) make yourself attack a Math question any faster than you are capable of attacking it.

With that all said, I would also advise that you generally don't time yourself when you are doing basically any ACT practice at home, regardless of the part of the test that you are working on. If you acquire the skills that you are capable of acquiring, then the clock will not likely be a factor for you on test day.

And now, having said that, I always want you to do what you ultimately feel makes you comfortable and confident. I just wanted you to know that the key to your success on test day will not be that you rigorously timed yourself at home over and over again.

2. Practice Tests

Along similar lines to where the last point left off, I also wanted you to know that the key to your success on test day will also NOT be that you made yourself take practice tests at home.

Why this is the case is pretty simple.

No practice test can really fully simulate the real day of the exam. For instance, taking a practice test online doesn't properly recreate the pencil and paper nature of the real exam. Taking a practice test from a book that doesn't contain actual ACTs that were actually administered does not properly recreate the real exam. Taking a practice test on a Sunday starting at 1:00PM most definitely does not properly recreate the real exam, which has a standard report time of 7:45AM.

Ultimately, there is no substitute for taking the real exam, and that experience, more than anything that a practice test could yield, is what is likely a key component to you achieving your best results.

③ *Just One Piece*

It really is true that your ACT score is only one piece of the overall college puzzle. Granted, it is a big piece and an important piece, but it is still only just one piece.

Your high school grades definitely really matter. The college essays that you will potentially end up writing really, really matter. I say this so that you understand that there is a balance that you can continue to strive to strike with your ACT prep.

Let me close this quick point I wanted to definitely make by acknowledging something else that also can give you a lot of peace of mind: there is no problem with taking the ACT as many times as you are up for taking it.

What?! Really?!

Ask me more about this if you don't believe me. But as an example, I worked with a student who took the ACTs more than five times. She ended up *choosing* to go to Duke, which if you don't know, is basically as tough a school to get into as there is.

④ *Find YOUR Path*

Ok, before we head off into the very final parts of this book, I wanted to sort of pull some things all together and remind you that your path to your dream isn't likely the same as your bff's path to her dream or his dream.

Let's say for instance that you are hoping to score a Composite of 30. Well, one way to achieve that goal would be to get an English score of 34, a Math score of 32, a Reading score of 24, and a Science score of 28. No college should care how you got that 30 Composite, so the fact that some sections pulled weight for the others is a zero issue.

It is the rare student who gets a Composite 30 because she actually gets 30s across the board. If you're not shy about sharing your scores, hit me up via Twitter with your subscores from your first real exam. I'll hit you back with what your best path might be to achieve whatever score you tell me you're hoping to reach.

There is a path out there for you my friend. LTSA is your guidebook. It's time to start to say goodbye.

Coming Soon: LTSA Live

Interested in seeing LTSA come to life?

LTSA Live is a 4-hour discussion designed to simulate all of the realities and rigors of a real ACT.

We will analyze all sections of the ACT, from Section1: English to the optional essay. All key ideas and strategies from LTSA will be put into live action, while throughout the discussion, students will be able to ask questions.

Everything that you can imagine about what the real day of an ACT is like will be dissected. The 4-hour length (which mirrors the real length of the ACT) of LTSA Live has been expertly crafted to give students a firsthand sense of what the real day of an exam will feel like.

LTSA Live encompasses all of the benefits of taking a practice test, such as conditioning you to what it feels like to perform at your highest level throughout the challenging duration of test day. But unlike the often passive experience of taking a practice test in which a student simply takes a test and checks to see his results, LTSA Live will dynamically unearth key adjustments that all students need to make. By the end of the event, students will have a clear sense of how to implement and execute all of the essential strategies detailed by LTSA.

There is no better way for you to know precisely how to take all that you will have learned from LTSA and translate it into an incredibly effective performance on test day.

If you are interested in attending an LTSA Live session in your area, email us at Requests@LearningToSpeakACT.com

Epilogue

I am excited to say that this is my second book! If you happen to be one of the many students who may have read or will read the first one, *Learning to Speak SAT*, you may notice that there are many similarities. This is because there are now many similarities between the two exams.

Now, let me be crystal clear in telling you that no college requires both. Let me also tell you that most students do not really seem to do that much better at one exam versus the other. That is not to say that you couldn't be one of those people who are naturally a bit better suited to crush the ACT. But the bottom line for most of us is that we simply need to choose an exam and then *choose* to get good enough at it to make whatever dream we are dreaming not just a dream.

There are parts of this book that are based on straight facts. But then there are other parts of this book that obviously are tied to patterns, ones that I have devoted my life to finding for you. Now a pattern is a pattern and not a fact. Silly thing to say, maybe. I think it's important to acknowledge, because you can know that I will constantly be monitoring the exam to confirm that certain patterns are still running near 100%. If there are changes to these patterns, I will let you know. I will let you know via QOTW, which you better already be doing regularly! And I will let you know with updated editions of *Learning to Speak ACT*.

I imagine that it might go without saying that you should be re-reading parts of this book. How much re-reading you do depends on what dreams you are trying to make real. I can assure you without hesitation that if you knew everything that was within this book, from cover to cover, you would destroy the ACT.

We're in this thing together. And obviously this isn't really goodbye. I'll be talking to you via QOTW. Stay focused my friend. We got this.

#OnlyHardWork
@chrisXcho

Endorsements

I asked a student once what his favorite type of music is and he said, "Nothing." That was one of the saddest moments of my life. I have a favorite everything. I have a favorite clothing brand: Adidas. I have a favorite vegan restaurant: Seed to Sprout in Fair Haven, NJ. I have a favorite falafel wrap: the Enlightened Falafel Wrap at Mendocino Farms. If you're ever in Santa Monica, it's right on Wilshire between 6th and 7th.

Ok, seriously, the main reason I started writing this Endorsements page is because I wanted to talk to you about the calculator you might want to have with you on test day. If you don't already have a go-to calculator, then I would strongly recommend that you purchase the ***TI-30X IIS***.

The TI-30X IIS has a fraction button that definitely makes certain Math questions easier to deal with. For example, if I had to plug in the mixed number 3 & 1/3, I could use the "A b/c" button and simply hit 3, then that awesome "A b/c" fraction button, then a 1, then that super awesome fraction button again, and finally another 3.

This calculator is less than $20. It is the model of calculator that I personally bring to every exam I take. It is the calculator I took to the May 6th, 2017 SAT, which I scored a perfect 1600 on.

If you regularly use a graphing calculator, and that's the calculator that you plan to bring with you on test day, I would still recommend getting this calculator. You are permitted to bring more than one calculator to the test by the way. So bring your trusty graphing calculator, but maybe have this compact little dude as well.

Oh, and I should mention, if you haven't already purchased the Official ACT Prep Guide that is produced by the ACT people themselves, you should totally do so. Other than *Learning to Speak ACT*, it is the best book to own to fully prepare yourself for test day.

Tomorrow I'm meeting a couple of super favs (love you Reilly & Car!!!!) for acai bowls at our fav place Melonhead in Sea Bright, NJ. I will walk there, because I will walk anywhere that is within a minimum of three miles to where I'm currently at. I'll be rocking my Havaianas, because that's the only brand of flip-flops I wear. I'll definitely be in Adidas shorts, and there is an exceptionally good chance that Malibu by Miley Cyrus will be blaring in my ear buds.

On that happy note, it's time to type my final lines here. Maybe we'll chat on Twitter. Until then, remember that we can make this process about hard work. Grind out your scores. Earn your success. Love every day. Hell yeah.